Creating with Generative AI

From Text to Code, Art, and Innovation

Hawke Nexon

Table of contents

Foreword

We are at the dawn of a new creative era—one in which artificial intelligence is no longer confined to research labs or the hands of a few elite technologists. Today, generative AI tools are enabling artists, developers, educators, entrepreneurs, and everyday people to build, imagine, and innovate in ways once considered the realm of science fiction.

This book, *Creating with Generative AI: From Text to Code, Art, and Innovation*, arrives at exactly the right moment. It doesn't just introduce the capabilities of large language models and generative tools—it empowers readers to use them. Whether you're designing your first chatbot, generating cinematic visuals from a prompt, or streamlining your workflow with smart automation, this book will guide you step by step.

What sets this work apart is its clarity and practicality. The authors make complex topics accessible without sacrificing depth. They walk you through real-world use cases, show you how to prompt effectively, build responsibly, and think critically about the future of co-creation with machines.

Generative AI is not just a technology—it's a new medium. And like any great creative revolution, it belongs to those who learn to use it with purpose. I'm confident this book will help you do just that.

Welcome to the future of creation. You're not just reading about it—you're building it.

– Anonymous

Preface

A.1 Why This Book?

Generative AI is transforming the way we create, communicate, and solve problems. From writing articles and coding software to producing visual art and composing music, tools like ChatGPT, Midjourney, Stable Diffusion, and GitHub Copilot are turning ideas into reality at unprecedented speed.

Yet with such power comes the need for understanding and skill. Many people encounter generative AI through short tutorials or viral examples, but few grasp the depth of its potential—or how to use it responsibly and creatively.

This book was written to close that gap.

You won't find shallow overviews here. Instead, you'll explore **practical workflows**, **real-world tools**, **structured frameworks**, and **thoughtful strategies** that help you do more than just experiment. You'll learn to build, design, and innovate.

Objectives of This Book

- **Demystify generative AI** concepts without oversimplifying

- Provide **hands-on guidance** for text, code, and creative generation

- Introduce the **tools, frameworks, and best practices** used by professionals

- Equip readers with **prompts, flowcharts, code, and case studies** to master the AI-creation process

This is not just a book about using AI. It's a book about **creating with AI**—with depth, intention, and impact.

A.2 Who This Book Is For (Beginners to Innovators)

This book is written for a broad but focused audience. Whether you're new to AI or looking to deepen your skills, you'll find value here.

Reader Type	How This Book Helps
Beginners	Learn the fundamentals, terminology, and basic tools of Gen AI
Creatives & Artists	Explore AI-driven workflows for writing, design, music, and visuals
Developers	Use APIs, write prompts, and build applications using Gen AI
Entrepreneurs	Discover how to build products, services, or startups with AI power
Educators & Researchers	Understand AI tools for teaching, curriculum, and prototyping
Innovators & Tinkerers	Push the boundaries of AI creatively, ethically, and experimentally

Tip: You don't need to know machine learning to create with AI—you just need the right map. This book provides it.

As you move through the chapters, you'll go from **understanding what generative AI is** to **harnessing it for tangible results.**

A.3 How to Use This Book Effectively

This book is structured to support both **linear learning** and **modular exploration**. Whether you're reading cover to cover or jumping to specific topics, here's how to make the most of it:

Read with Purpose

- **Start with foundational chapters** if you're new to generative AI.

- **Skim advanced sections** if you're seeking specific tools, workflows, or prompts.

Engage Actively

- Follow the **step-by-step tutorials** to build projects as you go.

- Use **flowcharts and tables** to organize your understanding.

- Modify and experiment with **provided prompts and code examples**.

Apply What You Learn

- Complete the **DIY practice sections** at the end of each chapter.

- Reflect using the **recap tables** to solidify knowledge.

- Revisit earlier chapters as your skills grow—layers of learning will unlock deeper understanding.

Use the Book as a Reference

This book includes many **tables, comparisons, and walkthroughs** for quick access. Treat it as a **toolbox** you can return to when building real-world generative AI applications.

Tip: Keep a project notebook or digital workspace where you save prompts, results, and lessons from your hands-on work.

A.4 Overview of Tools, Projects, and Skills Covered

This book spans a **wide range of tools and techniques** across text, code, and creative domains. Here's a snapshot of what's covered:

Key Tools Introduced

Category	Tools Covered
Text Generation	ChatGPT, Claude, Gemini, OpenAI API, Poe
Code Generation	GitHub Copilot, GPT-4 API, DeepAgent, n8n
Image Creation	Midjourney, DALL·E, Stable Diffusion
Workflow Tools	LangChain, Prompt Engineering Libraries, ReAct

Project Types Included

Project Type	Examples
Text Automation	Email writers, blog generators, summaries
Creative Writing	Poetry, scripts, character building
Coding Assistants	Auto-coding tools, bug fixing, chatbot dev
Design + Art	Prompt-based image creation, visual stories
No-Code AI	Automation flows using DeepAgent & n8n

Skills You'll Build

- Prompt Engineering (instruction design for AI)

- Text-to-Text & Text-to-Image generation

- Code generation and debugging using LLMs

- Workflow automation with no-code and low-code tools

- Designing ethical, explainable AI solutions

- Building AI-assisted applications from scratch

Flowchart: Learning Progression in This Book

Start
 |
 v
Intro to Gen AI Concepts
 |
 v
Prompting + Tools Overview
 |
 v
Hands-On Text & Code Projects
 |
 v
Visual & Creative AI Workflows
 |
 v
Automation & App Building
 |
 v
Advanced Innovation & Best Practices

Important: This book is designed to give you both the **practical tools** and the **creative mindset** to build confidently with AI.

Part I: Foundations of Generative AI

Chapter 1: What Is Generative AI?

1.1 Definitions, Scope, and Real-World Applications

Definition of Generative AI

Generative AI refers to a class of artificial intelligence systems designed to **generate new content**, such as text, images, audio, or code, based on learned patterns in data.

Tip: Generative AI does not just analyze—it creates.

Scope of Generative AI

Domain	Examples of Output	Tools Involved
Text	Articles, poems, emails, dialogue	GPT-4, Claude, Gemini
Code	Functions, applications, bug fixes	GitHub Copilot, GPT-4, DeepAgent
Visual Art	Digital art, illustrations, concept designs	Midjourney, DALL·E, Stable Diffusion
Music	Melodies, beats, full compositions	AIVA, Amper, Soundraw
Video	Short clips, video avatars	Runway, Synthesia

Key Characteristics of Generative AI

- **Data-Driven Creativity:** Learns patterns from large datasets.

- **Prompt-Based:** Generates output based on natural language input.

- **Adaptive and Contextual:** Tailors responses based on input and feedback.

- **Multimodal Capabilities:** Operates across text, images, audio, and code.

Real-World Applications

Industry	Use Case Example	Tool/Model
Marketing	Social media copy, product descriptions	Jasper, Copy.ai
Healthcare	Patient summaries, symptom triage	Nuance Dragon, Med-PaLM
Education	Essay feedback, lesson planning	ChatGPT, Khanmigo
Law	Contract generation, legal summaries	Harvey AI, CoCounsel
Entertainment	Scriptwriting, character design	Sudowrite, Midjourney

Note: Applications continue to evolve as models become more capable and customizable.

Flowchart: Basic Generative AI Workflow

User Prompt

|

```
        v
Model Interprets Input
        |
        v
Content is Generated
        |
        v
User Evaluates and Iterates
```

Key Takeaways

- Generative AI produces new content, not just predictions.

- It's driven by prompts and large-scale data models.

- It is already transforming industries from education to entertainment.

Practice Task

Exercise:

Write a short description of your favorite hobby using this prompt in ChatGPT or another LLM:

"Explain [your hobby] to a 10-year-old in a fun and simple way."

Reflect on:

- How creative or human-like was the output?

- What would you change in the prompt to improve the response?

1.2 History and Evolution: From Rule-Based AI to LLMs

Early AI: Rule-Based Systems

Era	Approach	Characteristics
1950s–1980s	Symbolic AI	Logic rules, expert systems
1990s	Statistical Methods	Probabilistic models, basic pattern matching

Important: These early systems lacked learning from data and generalization.

Machine Learning Revolution (2000s–2010s)

- Shift from hand-coded logic to data-driven models.

- Algorithms began **learning patterns from labeled datasets**.

- Rise of **supervised learning**, **neural networks**, and **deep learning**.

The Rise of Generative Models

Year	Milestone	Description
2014	GANs Introduced	Generative Adversarial Networks (Goodfellow)
2017	Transformer Published	"Attention is All You Need" paper by Google

2018	GPT-1	First generative pre-trained transformer
2020	GPT-3	Breakthrough in natural language generation
2022	Stable Diffusion	Open-source text-to-image generation
2023	GPT-4, Claude, Gemini	Multimodal, reasoning-capable LLMs emerge

Flowchart: Evolution of Generative AI

Rule-Based AI

  |

  v

Machine Learning (ML)

  |

  v

Deep Learning

  |

  v

Transformers

  |

  v

Generative AI (LLMs, Diffusion, GANs)

Summary Table: AI Evolution Timeline

Phase	Key Feature	Example Models
Rule-Based AI	Hard-coded rules	MYCIN, ELIZA

ML Era	Pattern learning	Decision Trees, SVMs
Deep Learning	Neural networks	CNNs, RNNs
Transformer Era	Self-attention models	GPT, BERT, T5
Generative AI Era	Content generation	GPT-4, Claude, Midjourney

Key Takeaways

- AI evolved from rigid rules to flexible, creative systems.

- Transformers laid the foundation for generative models.

- Today's AI can generate text, images, music, and more.

Practice Activity

Reflective Questions:

1. What are the major differences between GPT-2 and GPT-4?

2. How does the concept of "self-attention" improve generation quality?

Try researching one model from the timeline and summarizing its role in 3 bullet points.

1.3 Industry Case Studies: Education, Healthcare, Design

Case Study 1: Education

Scenario: AI-Powered Tutoring and Lesson Planning

Tool Used: Khanmigo, ChatGPT

Use Cases:

- Auto-generating quizzes and lesson plans.

- Personalized tutoring sessions.

- Essay review and feedback.

Example Workflow:

Teacher Inputs Topic
 |
 v
AI Suggests Lesson Objectives
 |
 v
Teacher Reviews and Customizes Output
 |
 v
Lesson Delivered with AI-Enhanced Content

Impact:

- Saves time for teachers.

- Improves student engagement through personalized content.

- Supports inclusive learning with adaptable explanations.

Case Study 2: Healthcare

Scenario: Clinical Documentation Automation

Tool Used: Nuance Dragon, Med-PaLM
Use Cases:

- AI-assisted patient summary generation.

- Dictation-to-text transcription for doctors.

- Decision support in diagnosis.

Table: Impact in Healthcare

Benefit	Details
Time Saving	Doctors spend less time on paperwork
Enhanced Accuracy	Reduces manual errors in records
Patient Communication	Simplifies medical language for patients

Challenge: Strict regulations (HIPAA), model bias, patient privacy concerns.

Case Study 3: Design & Creativity

Scenario: Concept Art and Logo Generation

Tool Used: Midjourney, Adobe Firefly
Use Cases:

- Text-to-image for mockups and brand concepts.

- Style transfer and moodboarding.

- Iterative prototyping with clients.

Flowchart: AI-Assisted Design Cycle

Creative Prompt
  |
  v
AI Generates Concept Art
  |
  v
Designer Curates & Edits
  |
  v
Client Feedback & Finalization

Impact:

- Accelerates brainstorming.

- Reduces iteration time.

- Inspires new creative directions.

Key Takeaways

- Each industry adapts GenAI to solve sector-specific problems.

- The combination of **human expertise + AI augmentation** leads to high-impact results.

- Understanding context and constraints is key to successful deployment.

1.4 Generative AI in Your Daily Life

Common Daily Use Cases

Daily Activity	AI Tool Involved	How GenAI Helps
Writing Emails	Gmail Smart Compose	Suggests phrases and completes sentences
Social Media Captions	Copy.ai, ChatGPT	Generates witty, on-brand captions
Entertainment Choices	Netflix, Spotify	AI-curated suggestions based on taste
Photo Editing	Adobe Photoshop AI Tools	Auto-removes backgrounds, enhances detail
Shopping Recommendations	Amazon AI Models	Suggests products based on prior activity

Note: You may be using GenAI features without realizing it.

Personal Productivity Tools

- **Notion AI:** Summarizes notes and drafts content.

- **GrammarlyGO:** Rewrites and improves text tone/style.

- **Otter.ai:** Generates transcripts and meeting summaries.

Mini Case: Everyday AI

Scenario:

A freelancer uses ChatGPT to:

- Draft client proposals

- Brainstorm social media content

- Refine emails with tone-based prompts

Result: Saves 4–6 hours per week and increases professionalism.

Flowchart: Generative AI in a Daily Workflow

User Task (e.g., Writing, Planning)

   |

   v

Prompt or Trigger to GenAI Tool

   |

   v

AI Suggests/Generates Content

   |

   v

User Edits and Finalizes

Key Takeaways

- Generative AI is already integrated into many consumer and productivity apps.

- Awareness of AI assistance helps you use it more intentionally and ethically.

- You don't need to be a developer to benefit from GenAI.

Practice Activity

Challenge:

Pick a tool you use daily (like Gmail, Canva, Notion).
Ask yourself:

- Does it include GenAI features?

- How can you better prompt it to improve results?

Try a new prompt and record the outcome.

1.5 Common Pitfalls & Best Practices

Common Pitfalls When Using Generative AI

Pitfall	Description
Vague Prompts	Leads to generic or inaccurate responses

Blind Trust in Output	AI may generate factually incorrect or biased content
Overdependence	Relying on AI without critical review weakens human creativity
Ignoring Licensing & Copyright	Some outputs may infringe on protected data or training content
Skipping Human-in-the-Loop Review	Automation without oversight leads to quality and ethical risks

Important: Generative AI is a **collaborator**, not a replacement for human judgment.

Best Practices to Maximize Effectiveness

Do	Don't
Be specific with context-rich prompts	Use vague or open-ended commands
Review and edit AI output carefully	Copy-paste AI text without checking
Understand model limitations	Assume the AI "knows everything"
Test and iterate multiple prompts	Settle for the first result
Use GenAI ethically and transparently	Hide AI use from collaborators

Tip: Use the "Prompt Sandwich" Technique

A method for structuring effective prompts:

[Instruction] + [Context] + [Expected Output]

Example:

"Write a formal email (instruction) to a potential client introducing our AI consulting services (context). End with a call-to-action for scheduling a meeting (output)."

Flowchart: Prompt Optimization Workflow

Initial Idea

|

v

Write Prompt

|

v

Run in GenAI Tool

|

v

Review & Edit Output

|

v

Refine Prompt Based on Results

|

v

Finalized Output Ready

Key Takeaways

- Generative AI is only as good as the guidance you give it.

- Ethical, clear, and well-structured prompts ensure meaningful results.

- Human oversight remains essential for quality, compliance, and creativity.

1.6 From the Expert: The Next Big Shift in Gen AI

Future Directions Predicted by Experts

Trend	Description
Multimodal AI	Integration of text, image, audio, and video generation in single models
Personal AI Assistants	Context-aware agents trained on your personal data and style
AI in Real-Time Collaboration	Co-creative writing/design tools in live environments
AI-Augmented Development	Code + architecture generation, deployment automation
Responsible AI Governance	More tools to ensure fairness, bias mitigation, and explainability

Quote from an Expert

"The future isn't just prompt-in, output-out. It's a conversation — continuous, adaptive, and contextually aware."
— Dr. Nina Velasquez, Head of AI Research, FutureFound Labs

Potential Impact Flowchart: Where GenAI Is Going

Today: Static Prompt-Response

```
        |
        v
Tomorrow: Contextual Multi-Turn AI
        |
        v
Next: Autonomous Creative Agents with Personalization
        |
        v
Future: AI-Human Hybrid Collaboration Ecosystems
```

Practice Reflection

Prompt:

Imagine it's 2027. You're using a next-gen GenAI agent. What task would you delegate to it? Write a short paragraph describing your experience.

Key Takeaways

- Generative AI is rapidly evolving toward **contextual, conversational, and autonomous systems**.

- Preparing for these changes means developing flexible, ethical, and creative AI skills now.

- Innovation will come from the **fusion of human intention and machine capability**.

Chapter 2: The Technology Behind It All

2.1 Neural Networks, Transformers, and LLMs

Concept Overview

Term	Description
Neural Network	A system of layers mimicking brain neurons to process and learn patterns.
Transformer	Architecture that processes sequences in parallel using attention mechanisms.
LLM (Large Language Model)	A neural network trained on vast amounts of text to generate human-like language.

How Neural Networks Work (Simplified)

Input Data
  |
  v
[Input Layer] --> [Hidden Layers] --> [Output Layer]
  | (Weighted nodes) |
  v   v
Feature extraction   Prediction or generation

Transformer Architecture at a Glance

- **Key Components:**

- **Self-Attention:** Assigns weight to each word in a sentence based on relevance.

- **Positional Encoding:** Maintains word order context.

- **Multi-head Attention:** Learns from multiple perspectives at once.

```
[Input Tokens]
    |
    v
[Embedding + Position Info]
    |
    v
[Multi-Head Self-Attention] -> [Feed Forward] -> [Layer Norm]
    |
    v
[Output Tokens]
```

What Makes LLMs Special?

Feature	Benefit
Trained on internet-scale data	Captures wide-ranging knowledge
Few-shot learning	Can perform tasks with minimal examples
Autoregressive generation	Predicts next word based on context, word by word

Example: GPT vs BERT (Table)

Model	Purpose	Directionality	Common Use Case
GPT	Text generation	Left-to-right	Chatbots, writing
BERT	Text understanding	Bidirectional	Search, classification

2.2 GANs, Diffusion Models, and Multimodal AI

Understanding GANs (Generative Adversarial Networks)

Concept: Two neural networks — a generator and a discriminator — compete with each other to produce high-quality outputs.

```
[Noise Input]
   |
   v
[Generator] --> [Fake Image] --> [Discriminator] --> Real or Fake?
           ^
       [Real Images (for comparison)]
```

Component	Role
Generator	Produces new data (images, audio, etc.) from noise
Discriminator	Evaluates if data is real or generated

Use Cases: Image synthesis, deepfakes, art creation.

Diffusion Models

Concept: Start with noise and gradually refine it into a coherent image or audio.

Pure Noise
 |
 v
Iterative Denoising Steps
 |
 v
High-Quality Image

Feature	Advantage
High quality output	Better detail, fewer artifacts
Slower generation	Requires more compute

Use Cases: Midjourney, Stable Diffusion, DALL·E.

Multimodal AI

Definition: AI that understands and generates across multiple data types — text, images, audio, video.

Example Tool	Modalities Handled	Application
GPT-4-V	Text + Image	Visual Q&A, caption generation
Gemini	Text + Code + Images + Video	Complex assistant tasks
CLIP	Image + Text matching	Zero-shot classification, search

Flowchart: Choosing a Model Type

```
Task Type
  |
  |---> Text-only? ------> Use LLM (GPT, Claude)
  |
  |---> Image generation? ---> GAN or Diffusion
  |
  |---> Multi-input/output? --> Use Multimodal AI (Gemini, GPT-4-V)
```

Tip: Match the model type to the modality of your task — don't use a hammer to paint a picture.

Practice Reflection

Write a short description of a creative project (e.g., a children's book, a music video, or a startup idea). Which model type would you use and why?

Key Takeaways

Key Concept	Summary
Neural Networks	Foundation of AI; learn patterns through layers
Transformers	Modern architecture enabling massive model scalability
LLMs	Specialized in text generation and understanding

GANs	Competing models for generating realistic visuals
Diffusion Models	Step-by-step refinement for detailed outputs
Multimodal AI	Blends data types for richer understanding and generation

2.3 Fine-Tuning, Prompt Engineering, and Inference

Fine-Tuning Overview

Definition: Fine-tuning is the process of training a pre-trained model on a smaller, task-specific dataset to specialize its output.

Term	Description
Pretraining	Large-scale training on general data
Fine-tuning	Task-specific retraining for niche performance
Transfer Learning	Reusing knowledge from one model/domain to another

Flowchart: Fine-Tuning Workflow

Pretrained Model
   |
   v
Domain-Specific Dataset
   |
   v
Fine-Tuning Process (Adjusted weights)

|
v

Specialized Model Output

Example: A GPT model fine-tuned on legal documents becomes a legal writing assistant.

Prompt Engineering

Definition: Crafting effective instructions (prompts) to get the desired output from a model.

Key Components of a Good Prompt:

- Clear instructions

- Defined format and tone

- Example inputs (few-shot prompting)

Prompt Engineering Styles Table

Prompt Type	Description	Example
Zero-shot	No examples	"Summarize this text."
Few-shot	With examples	"Here's an example:... Now do this one."
Chain-of-thought	Step-by-step logic	"Let's solve this step by step."
Instructional	Task-based command	"Write a cover letter for a web developer job."

Prompting Tip: Use Explicit Instructions

Bad Prompt:

"Tell me about climate."

Improved Prompt:

"Write a 3-paragraph article explaining climate change for high school students. Use simple language."

Inference in Generative AI

Definition: Inference is the process of generating output from a trained model without further learning.

Stage	Description
Tokenization	Input text converted to model-readable tokens
Model Execution	Model processes tokens through neural layers
Output Decoding	Tokens converted back to readable text

Flowchart: Inference Pipeline

User Prompt

  |

  v

Tokenization

  |

  v

Model Computes Output (Forward Pass)

  |

v

Decoded Output

|

v

Displayed Response

Best Practices

Do	Don't
Use clear, specific instructions	Assume the model knows your intent
Experiment and iterate	Copy/paste random prompts
Include examples if needed	Rely on generic phrasing

2.4 Tool Comparison Table: Model Types & Use Cases

Model Types Overview

Model Type	Key Feature	Ideal Use Case	Example Tools
LLM (Text)	Predicts next word in a sequence	Writing, chatbots, summarizing	GPT-4, Claude, Mistral
Diffusion	Gradual noise removal	Art generation, design	DALL·E, Stable Diffusion
GAN	Generator-discriminator framework	Realistic image/audio generation	StyleGAN, BigGAN
Multimodal	Cross-input processing	Image-text apps, assistants	Gemini, GPT-4V, CLIP

Code Models	Specialized for programming	Code generation, refactoring	CodeWhisperer, Copilot

Tool Snapshot Table

Tool	Model Type	Input Modalities	Use Case	Free Tier
ChatGPT	LLM	Text	Writing, brainstorming	Yes
Midjourney	Diffusion	Text	Artistic image generation	No
Claude	LLM	Text	Conversational assistant	Yes
DALL·E	Diffusion	Text	Image generation	Limited
Gemini	Multimodal	Text, images, code	Complex assistant tasks	Yes
Copilot	Code LLM	Text/code	Code completion in IDEs	No

Flowchart: Selecting a Model Type

What do you want to generate?

```
   |
   |---> Text ---------> Use LLM (e.g., GPT-4, Claude)
   |
   |---> Images -------> Use Diffusion (e.g., Midjourney, DALL·E)
   |
   |---> Realistic visuals -> Use GANs (e.g., StyleGAN)
```

```
|
|---> Multimodal tasks -> Use Gemini or GPT-4V
|
|---> Code ----------> Use Code LLM (e.g., Copilot)
```

Practice Activity

Pick a personal or business use case (e.g., resume writing, product design, portfolio creation). Use the tool comparison table to choose an appropriate AI model and tool. Justify your choice in one paragraph.

Key Takeaways

Concept	Summary
Fine-tuning	Specializes a base model for a specific task
Prompt Engineering	The art of writing effective instructions for AI
Inference	Running a trained model to generate responses
Tool Selection	Depends on task modality, purpose, and skill level

2.5 Common Pitfalls & Best Practices

Common Pitfalls

Pitfall	Explanation	Example
Vague Prompts	Prompts lacking specificity lead to poor or irrelevant results.	"Tell me about AI."
Ignoring Context	Models require context to produce relevant output.	"Explain AI" without defining the scope (e.g., AI in healthcare).
Over-reliance on AI	Relying entirely on AI output without human oversight.	Using AI-generated content without fact-checking.
Lack of Fine-Tuning	Not adapting models for specific tasks leads to generic results.	Using a general-purpose LLM for specialized tasks like legal advice.
Unrealistic Expectations	Expecting models to understand complex nuances.	Assuming AI can automatically provide perfect creative outputs.
Ignoring Biases	Models can reflect biases present in training data.	Using AI in hiring without addressing potential biases in the model's training.

Best Practices

Best Practice	Explanation	Example
Craft Clear, Specific Prompts	Define the scope and detail of the task.	"Generate a 500-word summary on AI in healthcare using the latest research."
Provide Context	Include relevant information for the model to process.	"This is a legal question about contract law in California."
Double-check AI Output	Always verify AI-generated content before using it.	Cross-check data or code with reliable sources.
Iterate & Experiment	Refine and tweak prompts to get the best results.	Test different prompt variations to see what works best for your needs.
Fine-tune for Specialization	Train models on task-specific data to improve precision.	Fine-tune GPT on medical literature for a specialized health assistant.
Monitor Biases & Ethics	Continuously assess for biases and ethical considerations.	Address bias when using AI in recruitment or content moderation.

Flowchart: Common Pitfalls & Best Practices

Start AI Process

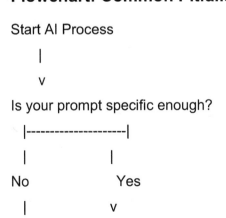

Is your prompt specific enough?

```
|--------------------|
|                    |
No                  Yes
|                    v
```

```
Refine Prompt        Is context provided?
     |                    |
     v                    v
Correct Pitfall     Continue to Process
     |
     v
Always Verify Output
     |
     v
Monitor for Biases
```

Key Best Practices Recap

Practice	Why It Matters
Specific Prompts	Ensure clarity and precision in AI outputs
Contextual Input	Improves accuracy and relevance of AI-generated content
Verification	Ensures AI does not produce incorrect or harmful content
Fine-tuning	Tailors AI models to specific industries or tasks

2.6 From the Expert: Why Prompt Engineering is the New Literacy

Expert Insight: The New Literacy

Generative AI has fundamentally transformed how we interact with technology. The ability to craft effective prompts is becoming an essential skill in industries ranging from marketing to software development. Expert [Name], a leading AI researcher, explains why prompt engineering is critical:

"Prompt engineering isn't just a skill—it's the new literacy. Just as we learned to read and write, the next generation must learn how to 'speak' to AI effectively. It's about framing your thoughts in ways that machines can understand, interpret, and generate valuable responses."

Flowchart: The Role of Prompt Engineering in AI Literacy

Learning AI Literacy

|

v

Understand AI Capabilities

|

v

Craft Effective Prompts (Start Simple, Then Refine)

|

v

Generate Relevant Outputs (via Inference)

|

v

Iterate & Improve (Refining Outputs and Prompts)

Why is Prompt Engineering the New Literacy?

1. **Expanding the Scope of Human Creativity**:

   o By mastering prompt engineering, users can push AI models to generate not only text but also art, music, code, and more, all tailored to their needs.

2. **Solving Complex Problems**:

   o The ability to craft nuanced and context-rich prompts opens the door to AI's role in solving complex, industry-specific challenges.

3. **Empowering Innovation**:

   o Businesses and creators who master prompt engineering can leverage generative AI to produce high-quality, cost-effective outputs—whether it's a poem, a business plan, or new product ideas.

Expert Recommendations for Mastering Prompt Engineering

Expert Tip	Why It Matters
Start Simple, Then Refine	Start with clear, simple prompts and add complexity as needed.
Test Variations	Experiment with different phrasing to understand model behavior.
Use Contextual Keywords	Adding specific context (location, audience, etc.) guides better responses.
Iterate Based on Feedback	AI learns with feedback. Adjust prompts based on what works and what doesn't.

Mini Case Study: AI-Assisted Writing

A writer looking to generate a blog post on sustainable living started with the prompt:

"Write a blog post about sustainable living."

After receiving a generic response, the writer refined the prompt to:

"Write a 600-word blog post about sustainable living practices for urban dwellers. Focus on energy-saving tips and eco-friendly commuting."

The output was more specific and relevant to the writer's audience.

Key Takeaways

Concept	Summary
Prompt Engineering	The skill of crafting effective inputs to guide AI outputs
New Literacy	Prompt engineering enables users to interact and leverage AI meaningfully
Iteration and Experimentation	Testing and refining prompts lead to better results

Chapter 3: Choosing the Right Tools & Platforms

3.1 OpenAI, Claude, Gemini, Mistral, LLaMA, and More

Introduction to Leading AI Models

In the rapidly evolving field of generative AI, several models are available that cater to different use cases. Understanding the capabilities, strengths, and limitations of each will help you select the right tool for your specific needs. Below is an overview of some of the top players in the generative AI space:

Comparison Table: Generative AI Models

Model	Creator	Primary Focus	Notable Features	Use Case Examples
OpenAI GPT	OpenAI	Natural Language Processing	High-quality text generation, fine-tuning available	Content creation, chatbots, summarization
Claude	Anthropic	Ethical AI, NLP	Designed for safety, focuses on ethical responses	Conversational agents, support bots
Gemini	Google DeepMind	Language, code, multimodal	Supports code generation, visual inputs, and more	Software development, cross-modal tasks

Mistral	Mistral AI	Text-based, open-source	Lightweight, fast models with fewer resources needed	Real-time applications, startups
LLaMA	Meta	Language processing	High efficiency, open-source, large-scale models	Research, language model training

How to Choose the Right Model for Your Task

Choosing the best model depends on your project's needs:

1. **For general-purpose content generation**, **OpenAI's GPT** models are highly versatile and capable of creating high-quality text in multiple domains.

2. **For ethical AI or safer responses**, **Claude** is a great choice, as it focuses on minimizing harmful biases and improving conversational integrity.

3. **For multimodal capabilities (e.g., text-to-image)**, **Gemini** from Google offers integrated support for both text generation and visual inputs.

4. **For resource-conscious applications**, **Mistral** and **LLaMA** are lighter, more efficient models that require fewer resources, making them ideal for real-time tasks or running on less powerful systems.

Flowchart: How to Choose the Right AI Model

Start

|

v

What is the Primary Task?

```
|------------------|
|                  |
Text Generation   Multimodal (Text/Image)
|                  |
v                  v
OpenAI GPT         Gemini (Text + Image)
|                  |
v                  v
Ethical Responses  Resource Efficiency
|                  |
v                  v
Claude             Mistral/LLaMA
```

3.2 Image, Audio, and Video Platforms

Generative AI isn't limited to just text-based tasks. Many platforms now allow creators to generate, modify, and enhance images, audio, and video content. Let's explore some of the top platforms available for these types of media.

Overview of Image, Audio, and Video Platforms

Image Generation Platforms

Image generation is one of the most exciting areas in generative AI, allowing artists, designers, and marketers to quickly generate high-quality visuals from simple text prompts.

Platform	Creator	Key Features	Use Case Examples
DALL-E	OpenAI	Text-to-image, inpainting, upscaling	Art, product design, marketing visuals

Midjourney	Independent	High-level artistic visuals, styles	Concept art, graphic design, illustrations
Stable Diffusion	Stability AI	Open-source, customizable, community-driven	Fine art, character design, creative storytelling

Audio Generation Platforms

AI platforms for audio generation are allowing for quick sound design, voice synthesis, and music creation.

Platform	Creator	Key Features	Use Case Examples
Jukedeck	Jukedeck Ltd.	Music composition, AI-generated music	Background music for videos, jingles
Descript	Descript	Text-to-speech, voice cloning, editing	Podcast creation, audiobook production
OpenAI Jukebox	OpenAI	Music generation with lyrics, various genres	Creative music production, music composition

Video Generation Platforms

The rise of generative AI in video creation enables automated editing, scene creation, and even full movie productions with minimal human input.

Platform	Creator	Key Features	Use Case Examples
Runway	Runway ML	Video generation, editing, and effects	Creative video production, special effects

Synthesia	Synthesia	AI avatars, video content generation	Corporate training videos, marketing content
Pictory	Pictory AI	AI-generated short videos, text-to-video	Social media videos, educational content

Choosing the Right Platform for Media

The choice of platform for generating images, audio, and video depends on the task at hand. Here are some general guidelines:

- **For Art and Illustrations**: Use **Midjourney** or **DALL-E** for high-quality, artistic visuals.

- **For Video Editing and Generation**: **Runway** and **Synthesia** are excellent choices, especially for generating dynamic video content with minimal manual editing.

- **For Music and Audio**: **Descript** and **OpenAI Jukebox** are great for generating music or audio content for podcasts, audiobooks, and more.

Flowchart: Choosing the Right Platform for Media

```
Start
 |
 v
What Type of Media Are You Creating?
 |--------------------|
 |                    |
Images          Audio/Video
 |                    |
 v                    v
DALL-E, Midjourney   Descript, Jukedeck
 |                    |
```

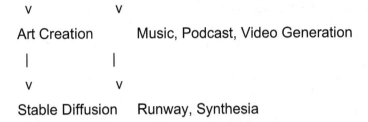

```
v              v
Art Creation      Music, Podcast, Video Generation
|              |
v              v
Stable Diffusion   Runway, Synthesia
```

Key Takeaways

Tool/Platform	Best For	Strengths
OpenAI GPT	Text generation	Versatile, high-quality content
Claude	Safe, ethical AI responses	Ethical considerations, fewer biases
Midjourney	Artistic image generation	Artistic and creative visuals
Stable Diffusion	Open-source image generation	Customizable, community-driven
Jukedeck/Descript	Audio creation and editing	Podcast, music composition, voice cloning
Runway	Video generation and editing	Video production, special effects
Synthesia	AI video content with avatars	Corporate, training, and marketing videos

3.3 SDKs, APIs, and Automation Frameworks

Introduction to SDKs, APIs, and Automation Frameworks

In this section, we'll explore key Software Development Kits (SDKs), Application Programming Interfaces (APIs), and Automation Frameworks that enable you to integrate generative AI models into your applications. These tools are essential for developers looking to create customized solutions or integrate AI capabilities into existing systems.

Understanding SDKs and APIs

1. **SDK (Software Development Kit)**: A collection of software tools and libraries that help developers build applications for specific platforms or frameworks. SDKs simplify the integration of complex systems like AI models.

   Examples: OpenAI SDK, Hugging Face SDK

2. **API (Application Programming Interface)**: A set of protocols and tools for building software and applications. APIs allow different applications to communicate with each other. For generative AI, APIs allow you to access pre-trained models and their capabilities.

   Examples: OpenAI API, DeepAI API, Google Cloud AI API

Key Features of SDKs and APIs

Tool/Platform	Type	Features	Use Cases
OpenAI API	API	Access to GPT models, fine-tuning capabilities	Text generation, chatbots, summarization
Hugging Face	SDK/API	Open-source models, easy integration, multi-modal support	NLP tasks, text-to-image, and more

Google Cloud AI	API/SDK	Pre-trained models, multi-cloud integration	Image recognition, speech-to-text, translations
TensorFlow	SDK	Popular machine learning library, AI model training	Custom model building, AI research
LangChain	Framework	Automation of workflows using LLMs	Building applications like chatbots, document search

Flowchart: How to Integrate AI via SDKs and APIs

Start

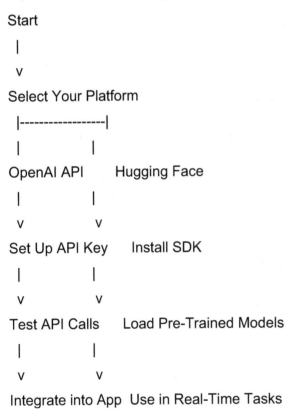

```
Start
 |
 v
Select Your Platform
 |-----------------|
 |                 |
OpenAI API      Hugging Face
 |                 |
 v                 v
Set Up API Key   Install SDK
 |                 |
 v                 v
Test API Calls   Load Pre-Trained Models
 |                 |
 v                 v
Integrate into App  Use in Real-Time Tasks
```

Automation Frameworks for Scaling AI Solutions

Automation frameworks allow developers to streamline AI workflows, enabling faster and more efficient integration of models into business processes.

- **LangChain**: A framework that helps automate AI tasks, especially when working with large language models (LLMs). Ideal for building chatbots, agents, and automation workflows.

- **n8n**: An open-source workflow automation tool that integrates APIs, including generative AI, for building automated tasks and pipelines.

- **Apache Airflow**: Primarily for orchestrating complex workflows, often used in data engineering but can integrate with AI for automating data processing and analysis.

Tool Comparison Table: SDKs, APIs, and Frameworks

Tool/Platform	Type	Key Feature	Use Case
OpenAI API	API	Text and code generation	AI-powered chatbots, text analysis
Hugging Face	SDK/API	Extensive pre-trained models	NLP, custom AI models
Google Cloud AI	API/SDK	Multi-modal AI, cloud support	AI for images, speech, and translation tasks
LangChain	Framework	Workflow automation with LLMs	Chatbot, document retrieval, AI pipelines
n8n	Framework	Open-source workflow automation	Integrating AI APIs into business automation

Apache Airflow	Framework	Orchestration for data and AI tasks	Automated data processing, scaling AI systems

3.4 Quick Tool Matrix: When to Use What

This matrix will help you quickly decide which tools to use for different types of tasks or projects. It will cover the right tool for your specific needs, from text generation to automation, image creation, and more.

Quick Tool Matrix: Use Case vs. Tool

Use Case	Recommended Tool/Platform	Why It Works
Text Generation	OpenAI GPT, GPT-4, Claude	Best for generating high-quality, coherent text
Image Generation	DALL-E, Midjourney, Stable Diffusion	Ideal for creating unique and artistic images
Multimodal AI (Text & Image)	Gemini, OpenAI, Stable Diffusion	Support for both text and visual inputs
Audio and Voice Generation	Descript, OpenAI Jukebox, Jukedeck	For voice synthesis, music generation
Custom Model Training	TensorFlow, Hugging Face, LLaMA	For building and training your own models
AI-Powered Workflow Automation	LangChain, n8n, Apache Airflow	Ideal for automating AI tasks and integrations

Flowchart: Quick Tool Selection

```
Start
 |
 v
What is Your Main Use Case?
  |--------------------------------|
  |                        |
Text Generation          Image Generation
  |                        |
  v                        v
OpenAI GPT, Claude         DALL-E, Midjourney
  |                        |
  v                        v
Detailed Content Creation   Artistic and Creative Visuals
  |
  v
Multimodal AI
  |
  v
Gemini, OpenAI, Stable Diffusion
```

Key Takeaways

- **SDKs and APIs** are essential for integrating AI into applications. Choose based on your task (e.g., text generation, image creation).

- **Automation frameworks** help scale AI tasks, streamline workflows, and integrate AI into business processes.

- **Quick Tool Matrix**: Always select the right tool for the specific problem you're solving, whether it's text, image, audio, or automation.

This section covers the essential tools and platforms you can use to build, automate, and scale your AI applications. The ability to choose the right tool will be critical as you dive deeper into generative AI and begin applying it to real-world problems.

3.5 Common Pitfalls & Best Practices

Introduction

Working with generative AI tools and platforms can be both exciting and challenging. While these tools offer immense capabilities, users often encounter common pitfalls when integrating AI into their projects. In this section, we will highlight the most frequent mistakes and best practices that can help you avoid them.

Common Pitfalls in Using Generative AI Tools

Pitfall	Explanation	How to Avoid It
Over-relying on default models	Using out-of-the-box models without customization often leads to suboptimal results.	Always tailor prompts and fine-tune models for specific tasks.
Inconsistent prompt design	Vague or poorly structured prompts lead to inaccurate or irrelevant outputs.	Be clear and specific with prompts, iterating on them until desired results are achieved.
Ignoring cost management	Using high-demand models for prolonged periods can become expensive.	Monitor usage regularly and consider using cheaper alternatives for low-priority tasks.

Data privacy and ethics issues	Generative AI models may unintentionally generate biased or harmful content.	Regularly audit outputs and ensure data privacy regulations are followed.
Neglecting model updates	Failing to update and fine-tune models results in outdated performance.	Keep models updated and use the latest versions of tools.
Assuming AI is infallible	AI-generated content can contain errors or biases that users overlook.	Always review AI output critically, particularly in high-stakes applications.

Best Practices for Effective AI Use

Best Practice	Explanation	How to Implement It
Prompt Engineering	Fine-tuning prompts ensures the AI generates more relevant and accurate responses.	Continuously experiment with different phrasings to improve output.
Model Fine-Tuning	Tailoring models to specific use cases improves their accuracy and performance.	Use available datasets to fine-tune pre-trained models on your domain.
Automation & Scaling	Automating repetitive tasks and scaling models helps streamline workflows.	Use frameworks like LangChain or n8n to automate routine AI tasks.
Ethical AI Use	Implement safeguards against harmful or biased outputs.	Regularly audit the AI's outputs, apply ethical guidelines, and train on diverse datasets.

Data Augmentation & Validation	Improve AI performance by supplementing training data and validating outputs.	Augment data with variations and ensure validation through real-world testing.
Documentation & Transparency	Good documentation ensures projects are reproducible and maintainable.	Write clear instructions, document code and model changes, and provide context for the AI outputs.

Flowchart: Avoiding Common Pitfalls

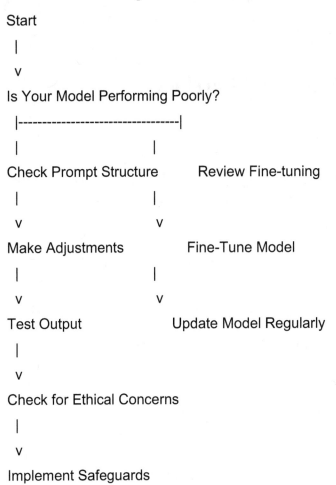

Start
 |
 v
Is Your Model Performing Poorly?
 |-------------------------------|
 | |
Check Prompt Structure   Review Fine-tuning
 | |
 v   v
Make Adjustments   Fine-Tune Model
 | |
 v   v
Test Output   Update Model Regularly
 |
 v
Check for Ethical Concerns
 |
 v
Implement Safeguards

Key Takeaways

- **Common Pitfalls**: Avoiding over-reliance on default settings, unclear prompts, and neglecting ethical considerations are key.

- **Best Practices**: Fine-tuning models, designing specific prompts, and automating tasks can enhance AI's effectiveness.

- **Continuous Improvement**: The world of generative AI is evolving rapidly; staying updated with models and tools will ensure optimal performance.

3.6 Career Pathway Highlight: AI Tool Developer

Introduction

AI Tool Developers are at the forefront of creating the systems, applications, and platforms that make generative AI accessible and practical for users. This section will outline the skills, tools, and steps needed to embark on a career as an AI Tool Developer.

Key Skills for an AI Tool Developer

Skill	Description	Tools/Technologies
Machine Learning (ML)	Understanding of ML algorithms and model training.	TensorFlow, PyTorch, scikit-learn
Natural Language Processing (NLP)	Ability to work with text data and language models.	Hugging Face, OpenAI GPT-3, BERT
Data Engineering	Building pipelines to process and clean data for AI.	Apache Kafka, Apache Spark, Pandas

Software Development	General programming skills to build scalable applications.	Python, JavaScript, Flask, Django
Cloud Computing	Familiarity with cloud platforms for hosting AI models.	AWS, Google Cloud AI, Azure
AI Ethics and Bias Mitigation	Understanding and addressing ethical concerns in AI.	Ethical AI toolkits, bias detection frameworks

Tools Used by AI Tool Developers

Tool/Platform	Purpose	Key Benefits
TensorFlow	Machine learning framework	Flexible, scalable, and widely used in AI development
Hugging Face	NLP model repository and platform	Provides pre-trained models for NLP and text generation
AWS/GCP/Azure	Cloud platforms for AI hosting	Easily scale AI models with powerful cloud resources
LangChain	Framework for LLM-based workflows	Automates complex AI workflows for developers
OpenAI API	Text generation, AI models	Access cutting-edge language models like GPT

Career Path: From Beginner to AI Tool Developer

1. **Step 1: Learn Programming**

   Start with Python, a key language for AI development, and understand basic programming principles.

2. **Step 2: Master Machine Learning & NLP**

    Dive deeper into ML algorithms and NLP techniques through online courses, textbooks, and hands-on projects.

3. **Step 3: Get Hands-On with Tools**

    Experiment with frameworks like TensorFlow, Hugging Face, and OpenAI API to build small projects. Start by generating text, images, or audio.

4. **Step 4: Build and Deploy Applications**

    Create scalable applications, integrate AI APIs, and work with cloud platforms to deploy your models.

5. **Step 5: Contribute to Open-Source Projects**

    Participate in open-source AI projects to collaborate with others, improve your skills, and build a portfolio.

6. **Step 6: Focus on Ethics and Bias**

    Stay up-to-date on AI ethics and bias detection, as these are critical aspects of modern AI development.

Flowchart: AI Tool Developer Career Path

Start

|

v

Learn Programming

|

v

Master ML & NLP

|

v

Experiment with Tools

|

v

Build and Deploy Projects

|

v

Contribute to Open-Source

|

v

Focus on Ethics & Bias

Key Takeaways

- **Skills Required**: AI Tool Developers need a combination of programming, ML, NLP, data engineering, and cloud computing skills.

- **Career Path**: Begin with programming and machine learning, then gain hands-on experience with AI tools, and advance by contributing to open-source projects.

- **Ethics**: As an AI developer, be sure to focus on the ethical implications of AI and its potential biases.

This section provides an in-depth view of the role of an AI Tool Developer, as well as the key steps to take if you're interested in pursuing this career. Whether you are just starting or looking to expand your skillset, there are a variety of tools and technologies that can help you advance.

Part II: Creating with Text

Chapter 4: AI-Powered Writing

4.1 Blogs, Articles, Poetry, Fiction, Screenplays

Introduction

Generative AI can assist in various forms of writing, from structured blog posts to creative poetry and fiction. This chapter explores how to leverage AI tools for different writing styles, the benefits of using AI, and the best practices for generating high-quality content in these genres.

Key Concepts

Types of Writing:

- **Blogs**: Informative, typically structured with headings and subheadings.

- **Articles**: Longer form, factual content that requires research and depth.

- **Poetry**: Creative and often requires rhythm, tone, and metaphor.

- **Fiction**: Creative storytelling with character development, plot, and theme.

- **Screenplays**: Structured, dialogue-heavy content with scene descriptions and character arcs.

Step-by-Step Guide: Using AI for Blog Writing

1. **Define Your Topic and Audience**

   - Example: A blog on "The Benefits of AI in Healthcare"

   - **Prompt**: "Write a blog post about the impact of AI in healthcare, focusing on its benefits for doctors and patients."

2. **Set the Tone and Style**

   - **Prompt**: "Create a conversational tone for the blog, targeting healthcare professionals and tech enthusiasts."

3. **Structure the Post**

   - Use subheadings for clarity: **Introduction, Benefits to Doctors, Benefits to Patients, Conclusion**

4. **Use AI to Generate Sections**

   - Start with an introduction prompt: "Write an engaging introduction on how AI is transforming healthcare."

   - Follow up with specific sections, such as: "Describe how AI is helping doctors in diagnosis."

5. **Edit for Quality and Accuracy**

   - AI-generated content should be edited for accuracy, tone, and coherence.

   - Use tools like **Grammarly** or **Hemingway** for grammar and readability checks.

Flowchart: AI-Assisted Blog Writing Process

Start

  |

  v

Define Topic & Audience

  |

  v

Set Tone & Style

  |

  v

Generate Introduction Section

  |

  v

Generate Key Sections (Benefits, Challenges, etc.)

  |

  v

Review & Edit Content for Quality

  |

  v

Final Draft Ready for Publishing

Step-by-Step Guide: Using AI for Poetry and Fiction

1. **Define the Type of Poem/Story**

   o Example: Write a poem on nature or a short story in a dystopian setting.

2. **Set the Mood and Tone**

   o **Prompt**: "Write a poem in a melancholic tone about the changing seasons."

3. **Generate the Content**

- Use an AI model like **GPT-4** to generate the text based on specific requests.

- Example for Fiction: "Write a short story where a detective uncovers a hidden truth in a small town."

4. **Review for Creativity**

- Ensure the poem or story meets the creative requirements: imagery, symbolism, or narrative structure.

5. **Polish and Edit**

- AI-generated fiction may need additional tweaking in terms of character development, dialogue, and plot structure.

Table: AI for Creative Writing Genres

Genre	Tools to Use	Key Characteristics	Best Practices
Blog Writing	OpenAI, Jasper	Structured, informative, SEO-focused	Use clear subheadings, keep paragraphs concise
Poetry	ChatGPT, Poet AI	Creative, emotional, rhythmic	Focus on tone, rhythm, and word choice
Fiction	GPT-4, Sudowrite	Narrative-driven, character development	Create strong protagonists and a clear plot
Screenplays	Final Draft AI	Dialogue and scene-focused	Stick to screenplay formatting, focus on dialogue

Articles	Jasper, WriteSonic	Long-form, factual, research-heavy	Ensure depth, check facts, provide clear conclusions

Best Practices for Using AI in Creative Writing

- **Use Specific Prompts**: The more specific your prompts, the better the AI-generated content will align with your intentions.

- **Refine AI Output**: AI writing tools are great at generating ideas, but they require human intervention for polishing and adding unique personal touches.

- **Avoid Overuse**: Don't rely too much on AI to generate entire pieces without human editing. AI should act as an assistant, not a replacement.

- **Maintain Consistency**: Ensure that tone, style, and narrative flow remain consistent throughout the piece.

4.2 SEO, Copywriting, and Branding Content

Introduction

AI-powered writing tools are especially valuable for **SEO, copywriting**, and **branding** content, where keyword optimization, persuasive language, and strategic messaging are essential. This section focuses on how AI can streamline content creation for these high-demand areas.

Key Concepts

SEO Writing:

- Writing content that ranks well in search engines.

- Requires attention to keyword usage, meta descriptions, and readability.

Copywriting:

- Creating persuasive content that motivates readers to take action (e.g., buying a product).

- Involves crafting compelling headlines, calls-to-action, and benefits-oriented messaging.

Branding Content:

- Content that communicates a brand's identity, voice, and values.

- Includes product descriptions, mission statements, and promotional material.

Step-by-Step Guide: AI for SEO Content Creation

1. **Keyword Research**

   - Use tools like **Google Keyword Planner** or **SEMrush** to find relevant keywords for your target audience.

2. **Craft SEO-Friendly Headlines**

   - Example Prompt: "Generate a headline for an article about the benefits of AI in education with the keyword 'AI education tools'."

3. **Generate SEO-Friendly Body Content**

   o **Prompt**: "Write an SEO-optimized paragraph on the use of AI in education, using keywords like 'AI learning tools', 'AI in classrooms', and 'future of education'."

4. **Meta Descriptions and Alt Text**

   o Generate concise and keyword-rich meta descriptions and image alt text.

5. **Proofread for SEO Readability**

   o Use tools like **Yoast SEO** or **Grammarly** to ensure the content is both readable and SEO-compliant.

Step-by-Step Guide: AI for Copywriting

1. **Define the Goal**

   o Example: "Generate a persuasive product description for a smartwatch that highlights features like battery life and fitness tracking."

2. **Create a Compelling Hook**

   o **Prompt**: "Write a headline that grabs attention for a blog post on the latest tech innovations in healthcare."

3. **Generate Persuasive Content**

   o **Prompt**: "Write a call-to-action encouraging users to sign up for a newsletter offering free AI resources."

4. Focus on Benefits

- ○ AI copywriting tools can quickly generate benefit-oriented messaging: "How AI improves productivity."

Table: AI Tools for SEO, Copywriting, and Branding

Tool	Purpose	Key Features	Best Use Case
Jasper	Copywriting, SEO	Content generation, tone adjustments	Ideal for blog writing, SEO articles, and copy
Copy.ai	Copywriting	Persuasive copy, CTA generation	Best for ad copy and email marketing
Writesonic	SEO, Copywriting	AI-generated content with SEO focus	Great for landing pages and product descriptions
Frase	SEO	SEO content optimization and research	Perfect for creating SEO-rich long-form articles
Rytr	Copywriting, Branding	Multi-language, brand tone consistency	Useful for short-form copy and social media posts

Best Practices for AI in SEO and Copywriting

- **Keyword Optimization**: Ensure AI-generated content includes relevant keywords without keyword stuffing.

- **Concise and Engaging**: SEO copy should be clear and concise; AI tools can help streamline this process.

- **Focus on Readability**: Ensure the content is easy to read and engaging; AI can help with sentence structure and grammar.

- **Brand Voice**: Customize AI output to match your brand's voice, ensuring consistency across all content.

Flowchart: AI-Assisted SEO Content Creation

Start
|
v
Conduct Keyword Research
|
v
Generate SEO-Optimized Content
|
v
Craft Engaging Headlines & Meta Descriptions
|
v
Review for Readability and SEO Compliance
|
v
Publish & Monitor Performance

Key Takeaways

- **SEO Content**: Use AI for keyword research, content generation, and meta descriptions to optimize for search engines.

- **Copywriting**: Leverage AI to create persuasive content, focusing on benefits and calls-to-action.

- **Branding**: Ensure your AI-generated content stays true to your brand's voice and message.

4.3 Story Structures & Prompt Templates

Introduction

In creative writing, structure is essential to engaging storytelling. Generative AI can help writers craft compelling narratives by following specific story structures and using prompt templates. This section explores how AI can assist in developing storylines, characters, and plot arcs, and how writers can use templates to ensure coherence and flow in their stories.

Key Concepts: Story Structures

Popular Story Structures:

- **Three-Act Structure**: Traditional storytelling model that divides the story into three acts—Setup, Confrontation, and Resolution.

- **Hero's Journey**: A common structure used in epic tales and myths, involving a protagonist who goes on an adventure, faces challenges, and returns transformed.

- **Freytag's Pyramid**: A model that breaks the story into exposition, rising action, climax, falling action, and resolution.

- **Seven-Point Story Structure**: A more modern approach focusing on key plot points like the hook, midpoint, and resolution.

Step-by-Step Guide: Using AI to Develop Story Structures

1. **Choose a Structure**

   - **Prompt**: "Generate a three-act story structure for a science fiction novel where humans discover a new planet."

2. **Create the Outline**

   - **Prompt**: "Provide a brief outline of key events in each act of the story: introduction, conflict, and resolution."

3. **Develop Characters**

   - **Prompt**: "Describe the protagonist of this science fiction story, including their background, motivations, and transformation."

4. **Plot Development**

   - Use AI to generate detailed plot points for each act or phase:

     - Act 1: Setup, character introduction

     - Act 2: Rising action, midpoint twist

- Act 3: Climax and resolution

Story Structure Flowchart:

Start
 |
 v
Select Story Structure (Three-Act, Hero's Journey, etc.)
 |
 v
Outline Key Plot Points (Introduction, Conflict, Resolution)
 |
 v
Develop Characters & Setting
 |
 v
Write Each Act or Section Using AI to Generate Details
 |
 v
Review, Edit, and Finalize the Story

Example of a Story Structure Prompt Template

- **Three-Act Structure Example**:

  - **Act 1**: "Write the introduction where the protagonist discovers a hidden artifact that will change their life forever."

  - **Act 2**: "Generate the rising action where the protagonist faces an unexpected challenge in their journey."

- ○ **Act 3**: "Write the resolution where the protagonist overcomes the challenge and returns home, changed."

Table: Comparison of Story Structures

Structure	Key Features	Best Use Case
Three-Act Structure	Clear beginning, middle, and end	Ideal for traditional storytelling, novels, screenplays
Hero's Journey	Focus on transformation and adventure	Great for epic tales, fantasy, and adventure fiction
Freytag's Pyramid	Focus on rising action and climax	Good for dramas, tragedies, and detailed storytelling
Seven-Point Structure	Modern approach with key turning points	Effective for concise plotting, short stories, and films

4.4 Co-Writing with AI: Human-AI Feedback Loop

Introduction

While AI can assist in generating content, the true value comes from **co-writing** with the AI, where both the human writer and AI work together to refine and enhance the output. This section explores how to establish an effective **human-AI feedback loop**, improving the writing process and ensuring high-quality content.

Key Concepts: The Feedback Loop

- **Initial Generation**: The AI generates content based on the writer's prompts, style, and structure.

- **Human Editing**: The human writer edits the output, refining style, tone, and factual accuracy.

- **Feedback for AI**: The human provides feedback to the AI to adjust its tone, structure, or creativity for the next iteration.

- **Iteration**: This process repeats, refining the content with each cycle.

Step-by-Step Guide: Establishing a Feedback Loop with AI

1. **Generate Initial Content**

   - **Prompt**: "Write the first draft of a short story about a mysterious island that appears overnight."

2. **Review and Edit**

   - Human writer reviews the AI output, checking for inconsistencies, narrative flaws, or style mismatches.

   - Example: "The dialogue feels unnatural. Rephrase it to sound more conversational."

3. **Provide Feedback to AI**

   - **Prompt**: "Rewrite the dialogue to make it sound more natural and relaxed."

4. **Iterate**

o   Repeat the process until the content aligns with the desired quality and tone.

Flowchart: Human-AI Co-Writing Feedback Loop

Start

|

v

AI Generates Initial Draft

|

v

Human Edits for Style, Clarity, and Accuracy

|

v

Human Provides Feedback for Adjustments

|

v

AI Rewrites Based on Feedback

|

v

Repeat Process Until Final Draft is Achieved

Best Practices for Co-Writing with AI

- **Be Specific in Feedback**: The more detailed the feedback, the better the AI can adjust its responses.

- **Combine Strengths**: Let AI handle repetitive or idea-generation tasks while focusing on creative or high-level decisions.

- **Use AI for Structure, Human for Creativity**: AI can generate outlines, scenes, and descriptions, but human writers should focus on character depth and emotional resonance.

- **Set Limits**: Don't let the AI take over the entire writing process. It should remain an assistant, not the primary writer.

Table: Best Practices for Co-Writing with AI

Practice	Description
Set Clear Boundaries	Ensure AI handles specific tasks, while humans manage the overall direction and creativity.
Provide Structured Feedback	Specific feedback helps AI make necessary adjustments.
Combine AI with Human Creativity	Use AI for ideation and structure, but keep creative control with the writer.
Refine with Iteration	Repeated cycles of editing and feedback ensure better quality.

Key Takeaways

- **Story Structures**: AI can help writers follow established story frameworks, ensuring a coherent narrative.

- **Feedback Loop**: The co-writing process between the writer and AI allows for continuous refinement of content.

- **Effective Collaboration**: By blending AI's efficiency with human creativity, writers can achieve high-quality results faster.

4.5 Mini Case Study: AI in Publishing & Journalism

Introduction

AI is transforming industries in ways that were previously unimaginable, and publishing and journalism are no exceptions. In this case study, we'll examine how AI is being used in these fields, from automating content creation to providing insights into audience preferences.

Case Study: AI-Assisted Journalism at Reuters

Scenario:

Reuters, a leading global news organization, has integrated AI to assist with both content creation and data analysis. Their AI-powered tool, **Reuters Tracer**, monitors social media and news platforms to detect emerging stories. Journalists can then quickly react to breaking news events and create articles with AI-generated drafts, saving time and ensuring they remain competitive in a fast-paced environment.

Key Insights:

- AI reduces the time required to create initial drafts, allowing journalists to focus on higher-level reporting.

- Natural language processing (NLP) is used to analyze text, ensuring the stories generated adhere to journalistic standards.

- AI algorithms can suggest headlines, summaries, and even quote relevant sources, reducing human error and improving the speed of news delivery.

Flowchart: AI Integration in News Creation

Start

```
|
v
```
AI Detects Emerging News Event
```
|
v
```
AI Drafts Initial Story Outline
```
|
v
```
Journalist Reviews, Adds Context, and Edits
```
|
v
```
AI Suggests Final Edits and Headlines
```
|
v
```
Publish

Case Study: AI for Automated Reporting in Sports Journalism

Scenario:

In sports journalism, companies like **The Associated Press (AP)** have adopted AI to automatically generate sports reports. AI systems use structured data (e.g., scores, player statistics, game highlights) to write quick match reports. Human editors then review the reports for accuracy and polish before publication.

Key Insights:

- AI can automate the writing of factual content like scores, which allows journalists to focus on in-depth analysis.

- The technology can scale the output, generating thousands of reports across different sports events, ensuring timely updates.

- AI ensures that reports are consistent, but humans are required to verify accuracy and add emotional or human elements to the stories.

Table: Key Applications of AI in Publishing & Journalism

Application	Description	Example
Automated Content Creation	AI generates initial drafts for articles based on structured data	Reuters Tracer, AP Sports
Audience Analysis	AI analyzes user data to determine content preferences	The Washington Post AI-driven recommendations
Content Personalization	AI customizes articles and advertisements for individual readers	Medium, NY Times
Fact-checking	AI tools help to automatically verify facts and sources	Full Fact, Factmata

4.6 Common Pitfalls & Best Practices

Common Pitfalls in AI-Powered Writing

1. **Lack of Contextual Understanding**:
   AI can produce content quickly, but without sufficient context, it may generate irrelevant or poorly understood output.

   Example:
   AI may generate a great blog post on "AI in healthcare," but without the right depth, it

could miss key ethical concerns, important medical contexts, or specific regulatory frameworks.

Solution:

- Provide clear, specific prompts with context.

- Use AI for ideation and structuring, but add your expertise for context.

2. **Over-reliance on AI**:
   Depending too much on AI can lead to generic content that lacks human creativity and emotional depth.

   Example:
   A press release generated purely by AI may be technically correct but lack the human touch that makes it compelling to readers.

   Solution:

   - Use AI as a tool for augmentation, not replacement.

   - Add a human layer of creativity, emotion, or insight where necessary.

3. **Bias in AI Output**:
   AI models can inadvertently perpetuate biases present in the data they've been trained on, leading to skewed or misleading information.

   Example:
   An AI-generated article on hiring practices might unintentionally reflect gender or racial biases due to biased training data.

   Solution:

- Regularly review AI-generated content for bias.

- Use diverse and representative training data.

4. **Inconsistent Voice and Tone**:

   AI can struggle with maintaining a consistent voice, especially over longer pieces of content or across different types of content (e.g., blog post vs. press release).

   Solution:

   - Set tone and voice guidelines for AI, particularly when using it across multiple platforms.

   - Human editors should harmonize tone and style to match the brand or publication voice.

Best Practices for AI-Powered Writing

1. **Set Clear Guidelines for AI**

   - Provide AI with structured prompts, clear instructions, and context to help it generate more relevant and targeted output.

   - Regularly update the training datasets to ensure AI models stay up to date with current trends, language, and biases.

2. **Focus on Human-AI Collaboration**

   - Use AI to handle repetitive tasks, such as research or generating content drafts, while humans focus on creativity, quality control, and adding nuance.

- The writer's role is essential for providing direction, ensuring accuracy, and maintaining a connection with the audience.

3. **Maintain Editorial Oversight**

   - Always review AI-generated content to ensure it meets editorial standards, adheres to facts, and aligns with the desired tone.

   - Human editors must verify the content's relevance and accuracy, adding value where necessary.

4. **Iterative Refining and Feedback Loops**

   - Use a feedback loop to refine AI-generated content. The more AI gets specific feedback, the better it will become over time.

   - Regularly update AI models to prevent outdated or inaccurate information from creeping into the content.

Do's and Don'ts of AI-Assisted Writing

Do's	Don't's
Provide clear, structured prompts	Use AI without context or purpose
Iterate and refine with AI feedback	Rely on AI for final drafts without human review
Set tone and voice guidelines	Allow AI to generate content without oversight
Collaborate with AI, not replace it	Ignore the potential biases in AI data

Key Takeaways

- **AI in Journalism**: AI helps streamline content creation, especially for time-sensitive and data-heavy tasks. However, human oversight ensures that content maintains quality, context, and relevance.

- **Common Pitfalls**: AI can generate biased or inconsistent content. Always review and refine the AI's output to avoid these issues.

- **Best Practices**: Use AI to augment, not replace, human creativity. Set clear guidelines, maintain editorial oversight, and keep refining the output for quality.

Chapter 5: Building Chatbots and Agents

5.1 ChatGPT, Claude, Rasa, Voiceflow

Introduction to Chatbot Technologies

In recent years, AI-powered chatbots have become a staple in customer service, personal assistants, and interactive user experiences. Chatbots use Natural Language Processing (NLP) and machine learning to interpret and respond to user input. In this section, we'll explore some of the leading tools and platforms for building chatbots and conversational agents: **ChatGPT**, **Claude**, **Rasa**, and **Voiceflow**.

1. ChatGPT

Overview:
ChatGPT is a conversational AI model created by OpenAI. It is based on the GPT (Generative Pretrained Transformer) architecture, which has been fine-tuned to handle diverse conversational contexts, making it highly versatile for various applications.

- **Strengths**:

    - Advanced NLP capabilities for natural, human-like conversations

    - Extensive API support for integration into different platforms

    - Can be used for a wide range of use cases, from customer support to content generation

- **Common Use Cases**:

  - Virtual assistants

  - Content generation

  - Customer service bots

---

2. Claude

Overview:

Claude is an AI model developed by Anthropic, with a focus on safety and ethical AI practices. Claude is designed for use in interactive agents that require thoughtful responses, and it emphasizes conversational clarity while minimizing bias.

- **Strengths**:

  - Safety-first design, focused on minimizing harmful outputs

  - Fine-tuned for high-level, conversational interactions

  - Adjustable "personality" for specific tasks or users

- **Common Use Cases**:

  - Education chatbots

  - Mental health support

  - Interactive user agents with a focus on trust and ethics

---

3. Rasa

Overview:

Rasa is an open-source framework for building custom conversational AI applications. It offers both **Rasa Open Source** for developers and **Rasa X** for team collaboration, making it a flexible choice for businesses looking to build scalable chatbot solutions.

- **Strengths**:

  - Fully customizable: build chatbots suited for your business needs

  - Integrates with messaging platforms and other tools via APIs

  - Supports machine learning-based intent recognition and dialogue management

- **Common Use Cases**:

  - Complex customer service automation

  - Integration with existing enterprise systems

  - Customizable assistant bots for niche business applications

---

4. Voiceflow

Overview:

Voiceflow is a platform designed specifically for creating voice-based conversational agents, such as Alexa or Google Assistant apps. It offers an intuitive, visual interface for building voice interactions without needing to write code.

- **Strengths**:

  - Drag-and-drop interface for building voice experiences

  - No coding required; ideal for non-technical users

  - Cross-platform deployment for voice assistants like Alexa, Google Assistant, and custom apps

- **Common Use Cases**:

  - Voice assistants

  - Interactive voice applications for customer service

  - Voice-enabled smart devices and IoT systems

Tool Comparison Table: Chatbot Platforms

Tool/Platform	Strengths	Use Cases	Ideal For
ChatGPT	Advanced NLP, human-like conversations	Virtual assistants, content generation	Developers looking for high-quality, flexible bots
Claude	Safety-first, ethical AI design	Educational chatbots, mental health assistants	Organizations focusing on safe and ethical AI interactions
Rasa	Open-source, customizable	Customer service, enterprise systems	Developers requiring full control and scalability

Voiceflow	Visual interface, no coding required	Voice assistants, interactive voice apps	Non-technical users, quick deployment for voice-based experiences

5.2 Context, Memory, and Personality Engineering

The Role of Context and Memory in Chatbots

A successful chatbot is not just about understanding input; it's about understanding **context** and **memory** over time. Building an effective conversational agent involves giving the bot the ability to remember past interactions, adjust based on user preferences, and manage ongoing conversations.

1. Context Management

Context allows a chatbot to maintain a coherent conversation. This can include understanding the **current topic**, **user sentiment**, **prior interactions**, and **intent**. Context is crucial for delivering relevant and meaningful responses.

Example:

- **Without Context**:
    User: "What's the weather today?"
    Bot: "The weather is sunny."
    User: "What about tomorrow?"
    Bot: "The weather is sunny."

- **With Context**:
    User: "What's the weather today?"
    Bot: "The weather is sunny."
    User: "What about tomorrow?"

Bot: "Tomorrow's forecast is partly cloudy, with a chance of rain."

2. Memory Management

Memory refers to the chatbot's ability to remember details between interactions. This is especially important for **personalized interactions**. A bot with memory can recall past preferences, names, or any information the user has provided in previous conversations.

Example:

- **Without Memory**:
  User: "I like hiking."
  Bot: "Thanks for sharing."
  User: "Recommend a good trail."
  Bot: "I found some hiking trails online."

- **With Memory**:
  User: "I like hiking."
  Bot: "Great! What type of trails do you prefer? Mountain or forest?"
  User: "Mountain trails."
  Bot: "Awesome! Here are some of the best mountain trails near you."

3. Personality Engineering

Creating a chatbot with personality involves programming the bot to **reflect a specific tone, style, and voice**. A bot with personality can make interactions feel more natural and engaging. This can be particularly valuable for branding or customer engagement.

- **Personality Traits**:

  - **Formal**: Professional and reserved (e.g., for legal, financial, or corporate use).

- **Casual**: Friendly and conversational (e.g., for social or entertainment apps).

- **Empathetic**: Caring and understanding (e.g., for healthcare or mental health bots).

- **Example**:

  - **Formal Personality**: "Good day, how may I assist you today?"

  - **Casual Personality**: "Hey there! How can I help you today?"

  - **Empathetic Personality**: "I'm really sorry you're feeling this way. Let's see how I can help."

Flowchart: Memory & Context Management in a Chatbot

User Input --> Process Context (e.g., Current Topic) --> Check Memory (previous interactions) -->

Bot Response (with context and memory) --> Store Context for Future Interactions

---

5.3 Integrating APIs, Actions, and Tools

Introduction to API Integration for Chatbots

Integrating external APIs and tools into a chatbot is essential for enhancing its functionality and ensuring that it can interact with other systems, retrieve data, and perform complex actions. API integration allows chatbots to access real-time information, interact with third-party services, and extend their capabilities beyond simple conversation.

---

1. APIs in Chatbot Development

APIs (Application Programming Interfaces) allow chatbots to communicate with external systems and retrieve information. For instance, a chatbot might use an API to fetch weather updates, make purchases, or fetch customer account details.

Example:

Weather API Integration:
A weather bot can integrate an API like OpenWeather to provide real-time weather data to users. The bot would send a request to the API, process the response, and provide relevant weather details.

```
import requests

def get_weather(city):
    api_key = "your_api_key"
    url = f"http://api.openweathermap.org/data/2.5/weather?q={city}&appid={api_key}"
    response = requests.get(url)
    weather_data = response.json()
    return weather_data['weather'][0]['description']
```

-

---

2. Action Integration for Automation

Actions are predefined tasks that a chatbot can execute. These actions might involve sending an email, booking a flight, processing a payment, or performing a database query. By integrating APIs, chatbots can automate these actions, ensuring efficiency and reliability.

Action Example:
A chatbot designed for booking appointments can integrate with a calendar API (e.g., Google Calendar API) to schedule and manage appointments.

```
import google_auth_oauthlib.flow
```

```python
import googleapiclient.discovery

def create_event(event_details):
    service = googleapiclient.discovery.build('calendar', 'v3', credentials=credentials)
    event = {
        'summary': event_details['title'],
        'start': {'dateTime': event_details['start_time'], 'timeZone': 'UTC'},
        'end': {'dateTime': event_details['end_time'], 'timeZone': 'UTC'},
    }
    event_result = service.events().insert(calendarId='primary', body=event).execute()
    return event_result
```

-

3. Third-Party Tools and Integrations

Chatbots can be enhanced by integrating third-party tools to provide specialized services. For example, integrating payment gateways, analytics tools, or customer relationship management (CRM) systems helps make chatbots more versatile and capable.

Tool Example: Stripe Payment Integration

A chatbot that helps users purchase products can integrate with payment gateways like **Stripe** to process transactions. The bot can guide the user through the purchase process and use the Stripe API to handle the payment.

```python
import stripe

stripe.api_key = "your_secret_key"

def create_payment_intent(amount):
    intent = stripe.PaymentIntent.create(
        amount=amount,
        currency='usd',
    )
```

return intent.client_secret

●

Flowchart: API Integration Workflow for a Chatbot

User Request --> Bot Receives Request --> Call External API/Action --> Process API Response

    | | |

    v   v   v

Bot Provides Response <-- Process Data --> Action Execution

---

4. Challenges in API Integration

1. **API Rate Limiting**: Many APIs impose rate limits to avoid overloading servers. Chatbots must handle rate-limiting gracefully and notify users if the limit is exceeded.

   Solution:
   Implement retries, back-off strategies, and communicate delays to users.

2. **API Security**: Handling sensitive information like user data or payment details requires secure API integration practices.

   Solution:
   Use **OAuth** for authentication and ensure that data is encrypted in transit.

3. **Error Handling**: API failures or downtime can interrupt chatbot services.

   Solution:
   Implement robust error-handling mechanisms and fallbacks in case an API is unavailable.

5.4 Mini Case Study: Healthcare Support Chatbot

Background

Healthcare is an area where AI-powered chatbots can greatly improve patient experience and streamline administrative tasks. A healthcare support chatbot can help patients book appointments, access medical information, track health data, and even get guidance on symptoms.

Case Study: Virtual Health Assistant

In this mini case study, we'll explore a healthcare chatbot built to assist patients with their daily medical needs, answer health-related queries, and provide remote consultation options.

Key Features of the Healthcare Chatbot:

- **Appointment Scheduling**: Integrates with a clinic's scheduling system to book doctor's appointments.

- **Health Monitoring**: Tracks health metrics like blood pressure, glucose levels, and more.

- **Symptom Checker**: Helps patients assess symptoms and suggests possible conditions or the need to see a doctor.

- **Medication Reminders**: Sends reminders for taking medications at the prescribed times.

API Integration for Healthcare Bot

1. Appointment Scheduling

The bot integrates with the **Google Calendar API** to schedule and manage appointments for patients. It checks the doctor's availability and sets the appointment.

2. Health Monitoring

For patients tracking health metrics, the bot integrates with **Fitbit** or **Apple HealthKit** to retrieve real-time data and store it in the user's profile.

3. Symptom Checker API

The bot uses the **Infermedica API** to allow users to input symptoms and receive potential diagnoses or advice. It integrates with this API to interpret symptoms and guide users on the next steps.

Example Code: Symptom Checker API Integration:

```python
import requests


def check_symptoms(symptoms):
    url = "https://api.infermedica.com/v3/diagnosis"
    headers = {"App-Id": "your_app_id", "App-Key": "your_app_key"}
    data = {"sex": "female", "age": 30, "symptoms": symptoms}

    response = requests.post(url, json=data, headers=headers)
    diagnosis = response.json()
    return diagnosis['common_diseases']
```

Challenges and Solutions in Healthcare Chatbot Integration

1. **Sensitive Data Handling**:

    Since health data is sensitive, strict security and data privacy standards like **HIPAA** (Health Insurance Portability and Accountability Act) must be followed.

    Solution:

Implement end-to-end encryption and secure authentication for user data.

2. **Accuracy of Health Information**:

   Medical chatbots need to ensure the accuracy and reliability of health advice.

   Solution:

   Use trusted medical databases (e.g., Infermedica) and continuously update the model with validated health information.

Mini Case Study Summary Table: Healthcare Chatbot Features

Feature	Tool/Platform Used	Purpose	Integration Example
Appointment Booking	Google Calendar API	Schedule doctor's appointments	Integration for availability check
Health Monitoring	Fitbit API, Apple HealthKit	Track and store user health data	Accessing health metrics
Symptom Checking	Infermedica API	Help diagnose symptoms and suggest actions	Input symptoms, get diagnosis
Medication Reminders	Custom Reminders System	Send reminders for prescribed medications	API for reminder notifications

Key Takeaways

- **API Integration**: Chatbots can be greatly enhanced by integrating APIs for real-time information retrieval and task automation.

- **Healthcare Chatbots**: Healthcare bots can manage appointments, health data, and symptom checking, improving the overall patient experience.

- **Security and Privacy**: When handling sensitive health information, ensure strict adherence to data security protocols, such as HIPAA.

5.5 Tool Comparison Table

In this section, we'll compare various tools and platforms that can be used for building chatbots and agents, with a focus on their unique strengths, use cases, and limitations. This will help you decide which tools best fit your needs based on your project requirements.

Tool/Platform	Key Features	Strengths	Limitations	Ideal Use Case
ChatGPT	Text generation, conversational AI	Versatile, high-quality language model	Limited context length, potential for hallucination	General-purpose chatbots, writing assistants
Claude	Conversational AI, customizable personality	High-quality language processing, customizable	May require fine-tuning for specific use cases	Customer service, personal assistants
Rasa	Open-source, customizable, supports dialogues	Highly customizable, supports multi-turn conversations	Requires more technical expertise for setup	Custom chatbot development, enterprise applications

Voiceflow	Visual interface for building voice and text bots	No code, easy-to-use interface	Limited by platform capabilities	Voice and text chatbot development for businesses
Dialogflow	Google-powered, supports NLP and integrations	Excellent integrations, robust NLP support	Requires Google Cloud setup	Building complex chatbots with NLP and integrations
Botpress	Open-source, highly customizable	Full control, multi-channel support	Requires technical skills for setup	Complex enterprise chatbots, internal apps
Landbot	Visual chatbot builder, drag-and-drop interface	User-friendly, no coding required	Limited flexibility for advanced customizations	Quick deployment of chatbots for websites and marketing
ManyChat	Automation for marketing and customer support	Built-in marketing automation features	Focused more on marketing, less on complex tasks	Marketing-driven chatbots, customer engagement

5.6 Common Pitfalls & Best Practices

Common Pitfalls to Avoid

Pitfall	Explanation and How to Avoid
Overcomplicating the Design	Chatbots should be simple and efficient. Avoid trying to build an overly complex bot with too many features. Focus on solving one key problem.
Ignoring User Intent	Not understanding or misinterpreting user intent can result in poor responses and frustration.
Overreliance on Pre-built Responses	Many platforms offer generic responses, but overuse can make your bot feel robotic.
Lack of Error Handling	Without proper error handling, chatbots may crash or provide meaningless answers when they encounter unknown inputs.
Neglecting to Update Content	Chatbots can become outdated if not regularly updated, leading to inaccuracies.
Security and Privacy Issues	Sensitive user data, like healthcare information or personal details, must be protected.

Best Practices for Building Effective Chatbots

Best Practice	Explanation
Define Clear Objectives	Determine the purpose and goals of your chatbot. Is it for customer service, support, or

	engagement? This will guide the design and functionality.
Focus on User Experience (UX)	The conversation flow should be intuitive and easy to navigate. Keep the interaction natural and avoid overwhelming the user with too many options.
Keep Responses Short and Clear	Aim for concise, direct responses that are easy for users to understand. Avoid long paragraphs and overly complex language.
Add Personalization	Use data like user name, location, or past interactions to make the conversation more relevant and engaging.
Integrate Multi-channel Support	Your chatbot should work across multiple platforms such as web, mobile, and social media to ensure broader reach and usability.
Test and Iterate	Regularly test the bot with real users and iterate on its performance. Gather feedback to continuously improve the experience.
Provide Human Escalation	In case the chatbot can't resolve an issue, allow for smooth handover to a human agent to handle more complex or sensitive queries.
Monitor and Analyze	Track user interactions, performance metrics, and other key data to understand how the bot is performing and where improvements are needed.
Use NLP for Better Understanding	Integrate Natural Language Processing (NLP) to enhance the bot's ability to understand user intent and respond contextually.

Ensure Accessibility	Ensure your bot is accessible to all users, including those with disabilities. Use voice input, screen reader compatibility, and other accessibility features.

Key Takeaways

- **Tool Selection**: Choose the right tool based on your needs, skillset, and the complexity of the chatbot. For simple chatbots, use platforms like ManyChat or Voiceflow. For more customizable and complex systems, consider Rasa or Botpress.

- **Pitfall Prevention**: Avoid common pitfalls like overcomplicating the design or neglecting error handling. Keep your bot simple, focused, and regularly updated.

- **Best Practices**: Prioritize user experience, ensure data privacy, and continuously test and improve the chatbot. Make sure to provide a clear escalation path for users to interact with a human when needed.

5.7 From the Expert: Voice Agents and the Future of Interaction

Introduction

The rise of voice agents is not just a passing trend—it represents a fundamental shift in how humans interact with technology. As AI systems become more advanced, the potential for voice-powered interfaces continues to grow. In this section, we'll hear from an expert in AI-driven voice technologies who will provide insights into the current state of voice agents and their role in the future of human-computer interaction.

Expert Insights: The Power of Voice in AI

- **Dr. Sophia Lee, AI Researcher at VoiceTech Labs**

  Dr. Lee has been at the forefront of AI-powered voice technologies, working on projects that integrate natural language understanding (NLU) with speech recognition and synthesis. She shares her perspective on why voice agents are a game-changer and how they are evolving.

The Future of Voice Agents:

"Voice agents are no longer limited to performing simple tasks like setting reminders or answering weather questions. With the advent of advanced NLP models, voice assistants are becoming more conversational, contextual, and capable of handling a wide range of user needs."

1. **Increased Personalization**

   Voice agents are rapidly improving in their ability to remember user preferences, tone, and context. As voice assistants like Siri, Alexa, and Google Assistant learn more about individual users, they'll be able to offer increasingly personalized experiences, tailoring interactions based on voice tone, speech patterns, and historical data.

2. **Multimodal Interactions**

   In the future, we will likely see voice agents integrate seamlessly with other forms of interaction, including text, visual displays, and even physical gestures. This multi-modal interaction will allow users to move fluidly between different methods of communication, enhancing the experience in ways that are intuitive and natural.

3. **Voice as an Interface for Complex Tasks**

   Voice agents are evolving beyond simple tasks and into complex decision-making processes. In industries like healthcare, voice agents can assist doctors by providing medical information, patient histories, and diagnostic support. Similarly, in business and tech, voice assistants can manage workflows, automate processes, and provide analytics insights through simple spoken queries.

4. **Emotional Intelligence**

    One of the more exciting developments is the ability for voice agents to detect and respond to emotional cues in speech. Through sentiment analysis and emotional tone detection, voice agents will be able to provide empathetic responses, which is crucial for applications like customer support and mental health care.

Voice Agents in the Real World: Industry Use Cases

Voice agents have found their place in a variety of industries, providing value in ways that were once unimaginable:

- **Healthcare**: Voice assistants are now helping doctors by offering hands-free access to patient data, clinical guidelines, and even remote consultations with specialists.

- **Customer Service**: AI-driven voice agents are handling more complex customer queries, reducing the need for human intervention and providing 24/7 support.

- **Smart Homes and IoT**: Voice-powered smart home devices are making it easier to control everything from lighting to appliances using simple voice commands.

- **Education**: Voice agents in education can provide personalized learning experiences by adapting to a student's needs and offering real-time assistance.

Challenges and Considerations

While the potential is immense, there are several challenges to be mindful of:

1. **Voice Privacy and Security**

    With voice-based interactions becoming more common, there's a growing concern over privacy. Voice assistants are constantly listening, which raises questions about how this data is stored and used. Ensuring user data is secure and providing transparency in data collection will be paramount.

2. **Handling Diverse Accents and Languages**

   Voice agents need to be capable of understanding a wide range of accents and dialects. As AI systems improve, so too must their ability to recognize and process diverse speech patterns to ensure accuracy across different regions and cultures.

3. **User Trust and Adoption**

   Despite significant advancements, many users are still hesitant to adopt voice technology due to concerns about data security and the accuracy of the technology. For voice agents to gain wider acceptance, companies will need to build trust through transparency, education, and consistent improvements in functionality.

Key Takeaways from the Expert

- **Personalization** and **context-awareness** will be key to the future of voice agents, allowing for more relevant, human-like interactions.

- **Multimodal interfaces** will allow for more seamless transitions between voice, text, and visual elements in interactions.

- **Emotional intelligence** will make voice agents more empathetic, especially for use cases involving mental health or sensitive situations.

- Challenges related to **privacy**, **security**, and **accessibility** must be addressed to ensure widespread adoption.

Conclusion

Voice agents are poised to become integral parts of our daily lives, making interactions with technology smoother and more natural. As the technology continues to evolve, the possibilities are limitless—from enabling hands-free workflows to creating intelligent companions that truly understand and respond to human emotions. The future of voice interaction is exciting, and it's only just beginning.

Chapter 6: Text Automation & Workflows

6.1 Email Automation, Summarization, Report Generation

Introduction

Automation is revolutionizing how we handle repetitive tasks, especially in business and professional environments. Generative AI tools have made it possible to automate complex tasks that were once time-consuming and prone to human error. In this section, we'll explore how generative AI is being used to streamline workflows like email automation, text summarization, and report generation.

6.1.1 Email Automation with AI

Email communication is integral to many industries, but managing inboxes can become overwhelming. AI-powered tools can help automate email responses, prioritize messages, and even draft personalized content. The ability to set up automatic replies, categorize emails, and summarize email threads is a game-changer for productivity.

Example Workflow for Email Automation:

1. **Inbox Prioritization:** AI tools can categorize incoming emails by importance or urgency based on content analysis.

2. **Automatic Drafting:** AI models can generate email responses based on previous emails and user preferences.

3. **Scheduled Sending:** Automate sending emails at specific times, optimizing outreach or marketing efforts.

Table: Email Automation Use Cases

Use Case	Description	Tools/Platforms
Automatic Email Categorization	Categorizes and flags important emails	Gmail with AI features, SaneBox
Personalized Drafting	Generates personalized replies for clients/customers	ChatGPT, Google's Smart Reply
Auto-Summarization	Summarizes long email threads	GPT-3/4, Grammarly

6.1.2 Text Summarization

Text summarization involves extracting key information from a large document or a series of communications, such as news articles, reports, or research papers. This process can save time and provide quick insights from lengthy documents.

Common Approaches:

1. **Extractive Summarization:** Extracts sentences directly from the document.

2. **Abstractive Summarization:** Rewrites the content to generate a concise version while preserving meaning.

Example Workflow for Text Summarization:

1. **Input:** A lengthy research paper.

2. **AI Processes:** Extracts the most important points and generates a concise summary.

3. **Output:** A readable summary that highlights the key findings, saving time for readers.

Table: Text Summarization Use Cases

Use Case	Description	Tools/Platforms
News Article Summarization	Condenses lengthy news articles	GPT-3/4, SummarizeBot
Research Paper Summarization	Extracts essential findings from papers	SMMRY, Paperpile
Meeting/Email Summaries	Condenses long meeting notes or email threads	Otter.ai, ChatGPT

6.1.3 Report Generation

AI-driven report generation can automatically pull data from various sources and generate reports with little to no human intervention. These reports can be personalized based on specific business needs, such as sales reports, customer feedback summaries, or performance analytics.

Example Workflow for Report Generation:

1. **Input:** Raw data from a database or spreadsheet.

2. **AI Process:** AI processes the data, analyzes trends, and generates a readable report.

3. **Output:** A comprehensive report with charts, insights, and conclusions, ready for presentation.

Table: Report Generation Use Cases

Use Case	Description	Tools/Platforms
Financial Report Generation	Auto-generates quarterly or annual financial reports	Microsoft Power BI, GPT
Customer Feedback Reports	Summarizes survey results and feedback for analysis	SurveyMonkey, ChatGPT
Sales Performance Reports	Creates detailed sales reports for business insights	Salesforce, Google Data Studio

6.2 Zapier, Make, n8n, and Custom AI Bots

Introduction

While automation platforms like Zapier, Make, and n8n can integrate various tools and trigger actions based on specific events, AI-driven automation offers more complex, customized workflows. By using custom-built AI bots, businesses can automate tasks with advanced decision-making capabilities. This section will explore how to build efficient workflows using both traditional automation platforms and AI-enhanced automation systems.

6.2.1 Understanding Automation Platforms

1. **Zapier**: A no-code platform that connects over 5,000 apps. It allows users to create workflows (called "Zaps") that trigger actions based on specific events, like receiving an email or creating a new document.

2. **Make**: Previously known as Integromat, Make offers a more visual approach to creating workflows, with advanced functionality such as conditional logic and multi-step

workflows.

3. **n8n**: A powerful open-source alternative to Zapier, offering custom workflows and integrations, as well as the ability to run workflows on-premises.

Table: Comparison of Automation Platforms

Platform	Features	Best For
Zapier	Simple UI, pre-built integrations	Non-technical users
Make	Visual workflows, advanced logic	Intermediate users
n8n	Open-source, custom workflows, self-hosted	Developers and enterprises

6.2.2 Integrating Custom AI Bots into Workflows

Custom AI bots add another layer of intelligence to automation workflows. These bots can handle more complex tasks like processing natural language input, recognizing patterns, and performing actions based on AI-generated insights. For example, an AI bot could manage email communication, trigger workflows, and even perform data analysis based on custom inputs.

Building an AI Bot Workflow:

1. **Input:** A user query or a new customer interaction.

2. **AI Bot Action:** The bot processes the input, searches for relevant data, and triggers subsequent actions.

3. **Output:** The bot sends personalized responses or triggers additional workflow steps based on the analysis.

Example Workflow:

1. **AI Bot** receives an email from a customer.

2. **Bot Processes** the email and identifies the query.

3. Based on the query, **Zapier** triggers a workflow to send the customer an FAQ document or create a support ticket in a system like Zendesk.

6.2.3 Automating AI-Powered Workflows with n8n, Make, and Zapier

By integrating AI with these automation tools, users can create advanced workflows that combine both automation and intelligent decision-making. For instance, using GPT-4 in Make or Zapier, you can auto-generate a response email, followed by a workflow that updates your CRM system with relevant data, and ends with sending a reminder for follow-up.

Table: Example AI Workflow Integration

Tool	AI Integration Example	Result
Zapier	Uses GPT-4 to generate email responses and triggers CRM update	Automated lead management
Make	Automates document generation with GPT-4, followed by email send	Automated reporting

n8n	AI bot processes data and triggers multiple app actions (CRM, email)	Multi-step automation

6.2.4 Common Pitfalls & Best Practices

Do:

- **Use conditional logic** for complex workflows.

- **Test automation flows** to ensure accuracy and avoid errors.

- Regularly **update workflows** to align with changing business needs.

Don't:

- Rely solely on out-of-the-box templates without customization.

- **Overcomplicate workflows** with unnecessary steps.

- Forget to **monitor automated tasks** for any system failures or issues.

Key Takeaways

- **Automation tools** like Zapier, Make, and n8n can help streamline workflows, but integrating **AI bots** takes automation to the next level by adding intelligent decision-making capabilities.

- **Email automation, summarization, and report generation** are common use cases for generative AI, improving productivity and reducing human error.

- **Best practices** include understanding the nuances of each automation tool and maintaining workflows that are scalable and adaptable to new business needs.

6.3 Interactive Knowledge Assistants

Introduction

Interactive knowledge assistants (IKAs) leverage AI and natural language processing to help users access, retrieve, and process information efficiently. Unlike traditional search engines or knowledge bases, IKAs can understand user intent, provide personalized responses, and even guide users through complex processes. In this section, we'll explore how to build and use interactive knowledge assistants for various business and educational applications.

6.3.1 What Are Interactive Knowledge Assistants?

Interactive knowledge assistants use **generative AI** to interact with users, answer queries, provide recommendations, and perform specific tasks. These assistants go beyond simple question-answering by employing contextual understanding and memory retention to offer more personalized interactions.

Key Components of IKAs:

1. **Natural Language Processing (NLP):** The ability to understand and process human language.

2. **Contextual Awareness:** Retaining the context of a conversation over time to provide more relevant answers.

3. **Task Management:** The ability to perform actions like scheduling, setting reminders, or retrieving data from various sources.

6.3.2 Use Cases for Interactive Knowledge Assistants

Interactive knowledge assistants can be used across various industries, such as **customer support**, **education**, and **enterprise knowledge management**. They can assist with anything from troubleshooting issues, answering FAQs, to offering personalized learning experiences.

Example Use Cases:

1. **Customer Support:** An IKA can manage customer queries, troubleshoot common problems, and escalate issues to human agents when necessary.

2. **Education:** In a learning environment, IKAs can help students by answering questions, providing study material, or guiding them through assignments.

3. **Enterprise Knowledge Management:** Employees can interact with an IKA to access internal documents, policies, and reports, saving time searching through knowledge bases.

6.3.3 Building an Interactive Knowledge Assistant

To build an IKA, you need to define its purpose, integrate the right AI models, and provide a user-friendly interface for interactions.

Steps for Building an IKA:

1. **Define Scope:** Determine what the assistant will handle — e.g., answering customer queries, managing calendar events, or providing study assistance.

2. **Select AI Tools:** Choose NLP models (like GPT, Claude, or LLaMA) and integrate them using APIs or SDKs.

3. **Create a Knowledge Base:** Build a structured database of information (FAQs, documents, user manuals) that the assistant can reference.

4. **Develop Dialogue Flow:** Design how the assistant will handle conversations, including follow-up questions and context retention.

5. **Deploy & Test:** Implement the assistant in a test environment, collect feedback, and continuously improve its performance.

Example Flowchart for Building an IKA:

Start
 |
 v
Define IKA Purpose
 |
 v
Select AI Model (GPT, Claude, etc.)
 |
 v
Create Knowledge Base (FAQs, docs)
 |
 v
Build Dialogue Flow
 |
 v

Deploy & Test

|

v

Feedback & Iteration

6.3.4 Tools for Building IKAs

There are various tools and platforms available for creating and deploying interactive knowledge assistants. Here are some popular options:

Tool Name	Description	Use Case
Dialogflow	Google's conversational AI platform	Building chatbots and assistants
Rasa	Open-source conversational AI tool	Customizable, on-premise assistants
Botpress	Open-source conversational platform	Deploying AI assistants for businesses
Microsoft Bot Framework	Comprehensive bot-building platform	Enterprise knowledge assistants

6.3.5 Best Practices for Interactive Knowledge Assistants

Do:

- **Maintain a strong knowledge base**: Continuously update the knowledge base to reflect the latest information.

- **Prioritize user experience**: Focus on making the assistant intuitive, with easy navigation and clear responses.

- **Incorporate feedback**: Use user feedback to iterate and improve assistant capabilities over time.

Don't:

- Rely too heavily on automated responses; sometimes human escalation is necessary.

- Ignore **context switching** in conversations, as it can lead to confusion.

- Forget to regularly **monitor and evaluate performance**.

6.4 Common Pitfalls & Best Practices

Introduction

When working with text automation, AI writing tools, and workflow automation platforms, it's crucial to understand the common mistakes people make and the best practices that ensure a smoother, more effective experience. By being aware of these pitfalls, you can avoid costly errors, optimize your workflow, and improve your AI-driven projects.

6.4.1 Common Pitfalls

1. **Vague Prompts & Instructions:**

- *Pitfall*: Providing unclear or ambiguous instructions to the AI, leading to poor or irrelevant outputs.

- *Solution*: Be specific and clear with your prompts, providing enough context for the AI to generate accurate and useful responses.

  - **Example**: Instead of "Write a blog post," specify, "Write a 500-word blog post about the impact of AI in education, including examples of how AI is used in classrooms."

2. **Ignoring Context and Continuity:**

- *Pitfall*: Overlooking the importance of maintaining context in longer conversations or workflows.

- *Solution*: Design workflows that consider context retention and coherence. In chatbots, always remember previous interactions.

  - **Tip**: Ensure your AI systems retain context in multi-turn conversations by tracking the conversation state and making responses relevant.

3. **Underestimating User Experience (UX):**

- *Pitfall*: Focusing too much on the backend (code and AI tools) while neglecting the user interface or interaction experience.

- *Solution*: A smooth and intuitive UX is critical for user adoption. Consider how your AI system will be used in real-world scenarios.

  - **Example**: Design your chatbot or assistant with easy-to-understand responses and ensure actions are clear (e.g., "Click here to schedule a meeting").

4. **Overreliance on AI Without Human Oversight:**

   - *Pitfall*: Allowing AI-generated content or processes to be fully automated without any human intervention, leading to errors, bias, or incomplete results.

   - *Solution*: Use AI as an augmentation tool, not a replacement for human oversight. Always ensure there is a review process in place.

     - **Tip**: Implement "human-in-the-loop" systems where critical decisions or reviews are handled by a person.

5. **Inconsistent or Outdated Knowledge Bases:**

   - *Pitfall*: Not regularly updating the knowledge base, which causes the system to provide outdated or irrelevant information.

   - *Solution*: Continuously update the AI's knowledge base to ensure accuracy. Implement a system to track updates and feedback to improve the assistant's performance.

     - **Example**: In a customer service chatbot, keep product information, pricing, and troubleshooting steps up to date.

6. **Lack of Personalization:**

   - *Pitfall*: AI systems that fail to provide personalized responses or experiences, leading to disengagement or user frustration.

   - *Solution*: Incorporate personalization techniques such as remembering user preferences, previous interactions, and customizing outputs.

     - **Tip**: Use AI's ability to personalize content based on user data, like location, interests, or past interactions.

6.4.2 Best Practices

1. **Clear and Specific Prompts:**

   - Always be clear, concise, and specific in your prompts. Providing the right amount of detail will help the AI generate high-quality output.

     - **Best Practice**: Use clear instructions, specify the tone, and provide context when appropriate.

2. **Consistent Testing and Iteration:**

   - Continuously test the output generated by AI systems. Prompt engineering and model fine-tuning are iterative processes that require refinement.

     - **Best Practice**: Regularly evaluate the quality of generated content or automation to ensure it aligns with the desired goals.

3. **Contextual Awareness and State Management:**

   - Ensure your system retains context across interactions. This is particularly important in multi-turn conversations or ongoing workflows.

     - **Best Practice**: Use tools or frameworks that allow context management, such as storing user history or session data for a more personalized experience.

4. **User-Centered Design (UCD):**

   - Focus on the needs and experience of the end-user. The interface and interaction design should prioritize simplicity, ease of use, and accessibility.

     - **Best Practice**: Use UX testing to refine user interfaces and ensure they are intuitive. Consider the user journey and streamline actions for the best experience.

5. **Human Oversight and Quality Control:**

   o Always implement human oversight where necessary. This is crucial for reviewing AI-generated content or ensuring workflows are functioning as expected.

      ▪ **Best Practice**: Set up review checkpoints in your workflow and provide options for human approval or intervention, particularly for sensitive tasks.

6. **Continuous Learning and Model Improvement:**

   o Regularly update your AI models and knowledge bases with new data to keep them current and improve their performance over time.

      ▪ **Best Practice**: Monitor user feedback, performance metrics, and domain-specific updates to iterate and improve the model.

Project Recap: Build a Personal Writing Assistant and Chatbot

---

Objective:

In this project, you'll integrate the principles and tools covered in this chapter to build a **Personal Writing Assistant** and **Chatbot**. These tools will be powered by AI to assist users with content generation (e.g., writing blogs, generating reports) and provide conversational interaction (e.g., answering queries, scheduling tasks).

Step 1: Define the Scope and Purpose

1. **Personal Writing Assistant**: Helps users generate content such as blogs, emails, or essays based on prompts. It should suggest edits and structure content efficiently.

2. **Chatbot**: Provides users with answers to common questions, integrates with external systems like calendars, and assists with simple tasks like making reservations.

Step 2: Choose Your AI Tools

- **Writing Assistant**: Use models like **GPT-4** or **Claude** for generating and editing text.

- **Chatbot**: Use platforms like **Rasa** or **Dialogflow** to handle conversational AI with multi-turn dialogues.

Step 3: Design the Workflow

Writing Assistant Workflow:

1. **Input Prompt**: User provides a topic or keyword.

2. **AI Content Generation**: AI generates a draft based on the input.

3. **User Review & Edit**: User edits the content, refining it.

4. **Final Output**: AI suggests improvements and formats the document.

Chatbot Workflow:

1. **User Query**: User asks a question or requests a task.

2. **Intent Recognition**: AI determines the intent and identifies the appropriate response.

3. **Action**: AI responds or performs an action (e.g., scheduling a meeting, retrieving information).

4. **Feedback Loop**: User provides feedback or makes a follow-up query, and the assistant remembers the context.

Step 4: Integration

- Integrate the writing assistant and chatbot with other tools (e.g., Google Calendar for scheduling, Grammarly for writing suggestions).

- Use APIs to link your assistant with external knowledge sources for real-time information retrieval.

Step 5: Testing and Iteration

- Regularly test both the writing assistant and chatbot by interacting with them and reviewing the quality of their output.

- Use feedback loops to improve the accuracy and usefulness of the generated content and responses.

By the end of this project, you will have a fully functional **Personal Writing Assistant** and **Chatbot** that can be deployed for a variety of tasks, demonstrating your proficiency with text automation, generative AI, and workflow design.

Part III: Creating with Code

Chapter 7: AI for Developers

7.1 GitHub Copilot, Amazon CodeWhisperer, Replit AI

Overview:

In this section, we will explore the tools available for developers to harness the power of AI in their development workflows. We'll cover some of the most widely used AI-powered coding assistants like **GitHub Copilot**, **Amazon CodeWhisperer**, and **Replit AI**. These tools can help you write, debug, and optimize code faster and more efficiently.

7.1.1 GitHub Copilot

- **What Is GitHub Copilot?**

  GitHub Copilot is an AI-powered coding assistant that suggests code and entire functions as you type. It uses OpenAI's Codex model to understand the context of the code you're writing and generate relevant suggestions.

- **Key Features:**

  1. **Code Suggestions**: Auto-completes code and suggests entire functions or lines based on the current code.

  2. **Context Awareness**: Understands the context of the code, including comments, variables, and functions.

  3. **Support for Multiple Languages**: Works with various programming languages such as Python, JavaScript, TypeScript, Ruby, and Go.

- **How to Use:**

  1. Install the GitHub Copilot plugin for your IDE (Visual Studio Code, JetBrains, etc.).

  2. Start typing code, and GitHub Copilot will suggest code completions.

  3. Use the **Tab** key to accept suggestions, or customize them as needed.

Example:

You're writing a function to calculate the factorial of a number in Python.

Code:

```python
def factorial(n):

  # GitHub Copilot suggests the entire function

  if n == 0:

    return 1

  else:

    return n * factorial(n-1)
```

-

7.1.2 Amazon CodeWhisperer

- **What Is Amazon CodeWhisperer?**
  Amazon CodeWhisperer is another AI-powered coding assistant, but it's specifically integrated with AWS services. It helps developers write code more quickly by suggesting

completions, code snippets, and even entire functions based on natural language descriptions.

- **Key Features:**

    1. **Integrated with AWS**: Provides specific suggestions related to AWS SDKs, services, and best practices.

    2. **Real-Time Code Suggestions**: Helps developers write functions, classes, and methods by suggesting completions as you type.

    3. **Natural Language Support**: You can describe your intent in plain language, and CodeWhisperer will generate the code for you.

- **How to Use:**

    1. Set up Amazon CodeWhisperer in your preferred IDE.

    2. Type comments or start coding, and CodeWhisperer will suggest possible completions or entire blocks of code.

Example:

You describe a function to interact with AWS S3:

Comment:

CodeWhisperer, write a function to upload a file to an S3 bucket

CodeWhisperer's Suggestion:

import boto3

```
def upload_to_s3(file_name, bucket_name):

    s3 = boto3.client('s3')

    s3.upload_file(file_name, bucket_name, file_name)
```

-

7.1.3 Replit AI

- **What Is Replit AI?**

  Replit AI is an integrated AI tool built into the Replit platform that assists developers in writing, refactoring, and testing code. It leverages large language models to offer code suggestions, debugging assistance, and even code completions in a collaborative environment.

- **Key Features:**

  1. **AI-Powered Autocompletion**: Replit AI assists in generating code suggestions, error detection, and fixing code as you write.

  2. **Multilingual Support**: Supports multiple programming languages and frameworks, including Python, JavaScript, HTML, and CSS.

  3. **Collaborative Environment**: Replit allows multiple developers to work on the same project in real-time, with AI suggestions enhancing productivity.

- **How to Use:**

  1. Start a new project on Replit.

  2. Use Replit's AI-powered autocompletion to receive code suggestions.

3. Utilize AI assistance for debugging, optimizing, and refactoring your code.

Example:

You're building a Python web scraper, and Replit AI helps with code generation.

Code:

```python
import requests

from bs4 import BeautifulSoup


def get_page_title(url):

    response = requests.get(url)

    soup = BeautifulSoup(response.text, 'html.parser')

    return soup.title.string
```

-

7.2 AI for Debugging, Refactoring, Testing

Overview:

AI is not only helpful for code generation but also plays a crucial role in the debugging, refactoring, and testing of software. In this section, we'll dive into how AI-powered tools can assist developers in improving the quality of their code by automatically detecting bugs, refactoring inefficient code, and suggesting testing strategies.

7.2.1 AI for Debugging

- **AI-Powered Debuggers**: Tools like **Sentry**, **DeepCode**, and **Codex-based debuggers** offer automatic bug detection. These tools scan your codebase for common programming mistakes, errors, and vulnerabilities.

- **How It Works**:

  - **Real-time Error Detection**: AI debuggers continuously analyze the code and highlight errors or inefficiencies in real time.

  - **Suggested Fixes**: AI-powered debuggers suggest fixes and improvements based on the patterns it recognizes in your code.

- **Example**:
  If a developer introduces a variable that is not used anywhere, the debugger will highlight this as a potential issue. It might also recommend a refactor or a more efficient way to structure the code.

7.2.2 AI for Refactoring

- **Code Optimization**: AI can help identify areas of your code that are suboptimal or redundant, suggesting more efficient ways of writing the same functionality.

- **How It Works**:

  - **Pattern Recognition**: AI tools analyze patterns in your code and suggest better ways of achieving the same results.

-     ○ **Suggestions**: These tools suggest removing unnecessary code, improving loops, and making better use of built-in functions.

- **Example**:

  AI might suggest converting a series of nested if-else conditions into a dictionary lookup, which could significantly reduce the complexity of the code.

7.2.3 AI for Testing

- **Automated Unit Testing**: Tools like **Testim** and **Mabl** use AI to generate and execute unit tests automatically. These tools can help ensure that your code works as expected by generating test cases based on code patterns.

- **How It Works**:

  -     ○ **Test Generation**: The AI analyzes your code and generates possible edge cases and test scenarios.

  -     ○ **Test Execution**: The AI runs these tests and provides reports on failed test cases and possible bugs.

  -     ○ **Suggestions for Improvement**: After running tests, AI can suggest ways to improve your code based on failures or inefficiencies identified during testing.

- **Example**:

  AI might detect that a particular function is not being tested adequately and will generate additional tests to ensure edge cases are handled correctly.

7.3 Tool Comparison Table: AI for Developers

Tool	Purpose	Supported Languages	Key Feature	Ideal For
GitHub Copilot	Code suggestions and completions	Python, JavaScript, Java, Go, etc.	Context-aware code suggestions, real-time collaboration	Developers of all levels
Amazon CodeWhisperer	Code suggestions for AWS integrations	Python, Java, JavaScript, etc.	AWS SDK & service-specific suggestions	AWS-focused developers
Replit AI	Code completion and debugging	Python, JavaScript, etc.	Collaborative coding and real-time suggestions	Beginner developers
Sentry	Debugging and error detection	Multiple	Real-time error tracking, bug detection	All developers
DeepCode	AI-powered code reviews	Multiple	Code quality checks, bug fixes, and suggestions	Professional developers

Testim	Automated testing	JavaScript, Java, etc.	AI-generated test cases and reports	Developers focused on testing

7.3 Mini Case Study: Startups Using Copilot

Overview:

In this section, we explore how startups are leveraging AI-powered tools like GitHub Copilot to accelerate development, improve productivity, and reduce development costs. We will look at real-life examples of startups that successfully integrated Copilot into their workflow and discuss the benefits and challenges they encountered.

Case Study 1: CodeAccel - A Fast-Paced SaaS Startup

Company Background:

- **Industry**: Software as a Service (SaaS)

- **Team Size**: 10 Developers

- **Tech Stack**: Python, JavaScript, React, AWS

Challenge:

CodeAccel was a growing SaaS startup with limited resources. Their developers were facing challenges in maintaining productivity while also scaling their product rapidly. They needed a way to increase code output without compromising quality.

Solution:

- The team adopted **GitHub Copilot** to assist with rapid code generation, bug fixes, and code suggestions.

- Developers used Copilot to accelerate the creation of new features and to automate mundane tasks, allowing them to focus on more complex problems.

Results:

- **Increased Development Speed**: Copilot allowed developers to write code faster by automatically suggesting code completions, entire functions, and boilerplate code. This led to faster feature releases.

- **Improved Code Quality**: Copilot's suggestions helped reduce errors and ensured adherence to best practices, resulting in cleaner code and fewer bugs.

- **Cost Efficiency**: With fewer developers on the team, Copilot helped optimize productivity, which kept operational costs low.

Takeaways:

- Startups can scale development without needing to increase team size drastically.

- Copilot's ability to assist with code completion and refactoring frees up developers to focus on more complex tasks.

- It's essential to review AI suggestions thoroughly, as Copilot may not always understand domain-specific requirements fully.

Case Study 2: DataFlow - An AI-Powered Analytics Startup

Company Background:

- **Industry**: Artificial Intelligence and Data Analytics

- **Team Size**: 15 Developers, Data Scientists

- **Tech Stack**: Python, TensorFlow, Docker, Kubernetes

Challenge:

DataFlow was focused on building cutting-edge machine learning models and deploying them as part of an analytics platform. Their data scientists and developers faced time constraints due to the complexity of AI model integration and deployment.

Solution:

- **GitHub Copilot** was used to assist in generating boilerplate code for model training, data processing, and deployment scripts.

- Developers relied on Copilot to help write testing scripts, set up CI/CD pipelines, and even integrate machine learning libraries.

Results:

- **Faster Prototyping**: Copilot helped the team quickly build prototypes for new features and models by automating repetitive tasks and suggesting best practices.

- **Improved Collaboration**: Copilot provided a consistent coding style and structure, making it easier for team members to collaborate on the same codebase.

- **Boosted Innovation**: With AI-powered assistance, the team had more time to experiment with new algorithms and fine-tune their models.

Takeaways:

- Copilot is useful for automating mundane coding tasks but should be used alongside domain expertise to ensure the generated code meets business requirements.

- It's vital for startups to integrate AI tools into their workflows where they offer the most value (e.g., code refactoring, documentation generation, and testing).

Case Study 3: HealthTech Co. - Building a Telemedicine Platform

Company Background:

- **Industry**: Healthcare Technology (Telemedicine)

- **Team Size**: 20 Developers

- **Tech Stack**: JavaScript, React Native, Node.js, MongoDB, Firebase

Challenge:

HealthTech Co. faced a tight timeline to launch their telemedicine platform and needed a way to speed up the development process while ensuring compliance with healthcare regulations.

Solution:

- The development team adopted **GitHub Copilot** to assist with coding front-end components, writing backend services, and managing real-time communications through APIs.

- Copilot helped generate regulatory-compliant boilerplate code for privacy and security features such as patient data encryption.

Results:

- **Faster Feature Rollouts**: The team quickly rolled out features like appointment booking, video conferencing, and patient record management.

- **Compliance**: Copilot's suggestions for handling sensitive data ensured the team adhered to HIPAA (Health Insurance Portability and Accountability Act) guidelines.

- **Reduced Development Overhead**: By automating repetitive tasks such as API creation and user authentication, Copilot significantly reduced manual coding time.

Takeaways:

- AI-powered tools can be crucial in highly regulated industries like healthcare, where code compliance is non-negotiable.

- Copilot can help automate critical tasks but requires diligent oversight for regulatory and security concerns.

Key Insights from the Case Studies:

- **Productivity Boost**: Startups in various industries benefit from using Copilot, with increased productivity and reduced development timelines.

- **Cost-Effective Scaling**: AI tools enable small teams to scale their product development without needing to hire additional developers.

- **Domain-Specific Expertise Required**: While Copilot can assist with many aspects of development, teams still need to have domain expertise to ensure the generated code meets specific business needs and compliance standards.

- **AI as a Productivity Partner**: GitHub Copilot acts as a virtual partner for developers, enhancing their productivity by suggesting code snippets, improving code quality, and reducing time spent on manual tasks.

7.4 Common Pitfalls & Best Practices

Common Pitfalls to Avoid:

1. **Over-reliance on AI Suggestions:**

   - AI tools like GitHub Copilot are powerful, but they're not foolproof. Blindly accepting suggestions without understanding the underlying logic can lead to errors, security vulnerabilities, or non-compliant code.

   - **Solution**: Always review the code before deploying it to production. Treat AI suggestions as a starting point rather than a final solution.

2. **Lack of Domain-Specific Fine-Tuning:**

   - While GitHub Copilot can generate code based on general programming practices, it may not always understand the specific requirements of your domain (e.g., healthcare, finance).

   - **Solution**: Customize and fine-tune AI suggestions according to your specific domain needs. Always ensure that the generated code meets business logic, regulatory standards, and performance requirements.

3. **Ignoring Security and Privacy Concerns:**

   - AI models do not inherently prioritize security or privacy considerations, which can be crucial, especially in sensitive industries like healthcare or finance.

- **Solution**: Make sure to manually incorporate best practices for secure coding and compliance into your development process. Use AI tools to assist, but always perform a security audit of the generated code.

4. **Underestimating the Need for Human Oversight:**

   - AI tools are best when used as a supplement to human expertise, not a replacement. It's easy to fall into the trap of assuming that AI-generated code is perfect or complete.

   - **Solution**: Maintain human oversight in all stages of development. Ensure that AI suggestions are verified, integrated properly, and reviewed for quality.

Best Practices for AI-Assisted Development:

1. **Start Simple and Gradually Increase Complexity:**

   - Begin by using AI tools for simpler, repetitive tasks like code formatting, auto-completion, and boilerplate generation. As you gain confidence, use AI to assist with more complex tasks like refactoring or debugging.

2. **Integrate AI into Existing Workflows:**

   - To get the most value from tools like GitHub Copilot, integrate them directly into your existing development environment and workflow. This reduces friction and makes AI a seamless part of your daily routine.

3. **Encourage Collaboration Between AI and Developers:**

   - Use AI as a collaborator rather than a tool. Encourage your developers to interact with Copilot, ask for alternative suggestions, and even modify the generated code to fit specific needs.

4. **Set Up Code Reviews for AI-Generated Code:**

   - Establish a code review process specifically for AI-generated code. This ensures that any potential issues (bugs, inefficiencies, or security risks) are caught before deployment.

5. **Continuously Learn and Adapt:**

   - AI tools are continuously improving. Keep up with the latest features, updates, and best practices to ensure that you're getting the most out of your AI-powered coding assistant.

7.5 Career Spotlight: AI-Augmented Developer

Overview:

The role of the developer is evolving, with AI tools like GitHub Copilot becoming integral parts of daily workflows. The **AI-Augmented Developer** is a new breed of software engineer who works alongside AI assistants to enhance productivity, improve code quality, and accelerate the development cycle. This career spotlight explores what it means to be an AI-Augmented Developer, the skills required, and how AI tools are reshaping the future of software development.

What is an AI-Augmented Developer?

An **AI-Augmented Developer** is a developer who uses artificial intelligence tools to enhance their coding practices, automate repetitive tasks, and improve code quality. These developers seamlessly integrate AI tools like Copilot, automated debugging systems, and intelligent refactoring assistants into their workflows, allowing them to focus more on high-level problem-solving and less on mundane coding tasks.

Key Characteristics of AI-Augmented Developers:

- Proficient in using AI tools for code generation, bug fixing, testing, and optimization.

- Able to collaborate with AI to create more sophisticated code while ensuring it aligns with business requirements.

- Skilled in the human-AI feedback loop, continuously improving and customizing AI suggestions.

- Capable of handling complex projects, leveraging AI to accelerate development without compromising on quality.

Core Skills of an AI-Augmented Developer:

1. **Proficiency with AI Tools and Frameworks:**

   - Understanding how to use AI-powered coding assistants like GitHub Copilot, Amazon CodeWhisperer, and AI-driven debugging tools.

   - Familiarity with AI libraries and platforms that support custom AI model integration (e.g., TensorFlow, PyTorch, OpenAI API).

2. **Advanced Programming Knowledge:**

   - Expertise in multiple programming languages (Python, JavaScript, Java, etc.), as AI tools can be language-agnostic, and different languages might be better suited for various tasks.

- Strong foundation in algorithms, data structures, and software architecture.

3. **AI-Driven Testing and Debugging:**

   - Ability to utilize AI tools for automated testing, code refactoring, and bug fixing.

   - Proficiency in using AI-assisted debugging tools like Replit AI or DeepCode to find issues and propose improvements.

4. **Effective Prompt Engineering:**

   - Crafting well-defined prompts and providing clear instructions to AI models for accurate code generation.

   - Understanding how to adjust AI's responses through iterative feedback to refine outputs for specific tasks.

5. **Collaboration and Code Review:**

   - Collaboration between human developers and AI requires a keen eye for quality assurance. AI-Augmented Developers need to review and refine AI-generated code for issues that may not be immediately apparent.

   - Building a continuous feedback loop with AI to improve results over time.

6. **Knowledge of Ethical AI Use:**

   - Understanding ethical considerations related to AI usage, including privacy, fairness, and bias in AI-generated code.

   - Ensuring AI tools comply with company standards and regulatory guidelines (e.g., GDPR, HIPAA).

Daily Responsibilities of an AI-Augmented Developer:

1. **Code Generation:**

   - Use AI tools like GitHub Copilot to generate boilerplate code, functions, and entire modules based on initial specifications.

   - Enhance productivity by letting AI handle repetitive tasks like writing documentation, comments, and standard functions.

2. **Code Review and Optimization:**

   - Review AI-generated code for logic, style, and performance issues. The AI-Augmented Developer refines the code, ensuring that it meets coding standards and business requirements.

   - Use AI to suggest code optimizations, such as refactoring, to make code more efficient.

3. **Debugging and Issue Resolution:**

   - Leverage AI-powered tools to automate debugging and identify performance bottlenecks or bugs.

   - Collaborate with AI to fix issues faster, allowing more time for innovation and higher-level problem-solving.

4. **Collaborating with Other Teams:**

   - Work closely with data scientists, product managers, and other developers to integrate AI-generated code into the broader project. AI-Augmented Developers facilitate communication between teams by automating some of the coding process and enhancing collaboration.

- Provide feedback to AI systems to improve their future outputs based on project needs.

5. **Innovation and Experimentation:**

   - Experiment with new AI tools, methods, and programming paradigms to improve development workflows and explore emerging technologies.

   - Implement AI-driven solutions in new projects, testing different AI platforms and refining tools for specific tasks.

Career Pathways and Opportunities:

As AI tools like GitHub Copilot and other coding assistants continue to evolve, the demand for AI-Augmented Developers is likely to grow. Developers can specialize in various domains or roles that leverage AI technologies, including:

1. **AI Software Engineer:**

   - Develop software that integrates AI systems into larger applications, enabling businesses to benefit from AI-enhanced functionality.

2. **AI Researcher/Engineer:**

   - Explore new AI algorithms and techniques to enhance the capabilities of AI-driven development tools. This could involve research in neural networks, natural language processing, or automated reasoning.

3. **AI Tool Developer:**

   - Build AI tools and frameworks that empower other developers. This role could involve creating new platforms for code generation, testing, and collaboration that integrate seamlessly into developers' workflows.

4. **AI Product Manager:**

   o Oversee the development of AI-based products and services. This role involves working closely with engineers to define product requirements, track progress, and ensure that AI tools meet users' needs.

5. **AI Ethics Specialist:**

   o As AI continues to grow, there will be increasing demand for specialists who understand the ethical implications of AI usage. These experts will ensure that AI development aligns with legal, moral, and societal standards.

Education and Training for AI-Augmented Developers:

To pursue a career as an AI-Augmented Developer, the following educational paths and resources are helpful:

- **Formal Education**:

  o A degree in **Computer Science**, **Software Engineering**, or **AI-focused programs**.

  o Specialization in **Machine Learning**, **Natural Language Processing**, and **Software Development** can provide the technical foundation needed to excel.

- **Certifications and Online Courses**:

  o Online platforms like **Coursera**, **Udacity**, and **edX** offer courses on **AI**, **Machine Learning**, and **AI Tool Development**.

- AI tool-specific certifications (e.g., **GitHub Copilot Developer Certification, OpenAI API Certification**) can enhance career prospects.

- **On-the-Job Learning**:

  - Start using AI coding assistants in personal projects or on open-source contributions to gain hands-on experience.

  - Join developer communities, attend AI-focused conferences, and engage in continuous learning to stay ahead in the field.

Salary Insights for AI-Augmented Developers:

AI-Augmented Developers are in high demand, and salaries are competitive across various industries. According to recent data, the average salary range for AI-driven developer roles includes:

- **AI Software Engineer**: $100,000 - $180,000 per year

- **AI Researcher**: $120,000 - $200,000 per year

- **AI Product Manager**: $130,000 - $220,000 per year

- **AI Ethics Specialist**: $110,000 - $170,000 per year

Salaries vary depending on location, experience, and the specific industry, but the field continues to grow rapidly.

Key Takeaways:

- **AI-Augmented Developers** are redefining the role of traditional developers by working alongside AI to increase productivity, reduce time-to-market, and create innovative software solutions.

- Key skills for this career include proficiency with AI tools, coding expertise, ethical awareness, and collaboration.

- The demand for AI-Augmented Developers is expected to rise, offering exciting career prospects and opportunities in multiple sectors.

Chapter 8: No-Code, Low-Code with AI

8.1 Tools: Glide, Bubble, n8n, DeepAgent

Introduction to No-Code/Low-Code AI Platforms

The rise of no-code and low-code platforms has democratized the creation of applications, enabling non-developers to leverage the power of AI for building innovative tools. These platforms abstract away much of the complexity of coding and offer visual interfaces, allowing users to build functional applications through drag-and-drop features, minimal programming, and AI-driven automation.

This section explores some of the most prominent no-code/low-code tools that integrate AI, including **Glide**, **Bubble**, **n8n**, and **DeepAgent**. These tools enable users to harness AI for various applications, including **automation**, **data analysis**, **workflow optimization**, and even **AI-powered app development**.

Glide

- **Purpose**: Glide allows users to create mobile apps without coding, turning Google Sheets or Excel files into fully functional mobile applications.

- **AI Features**: Glide incorporates AI-powered templates and data analysis features that make it easy to organize, display, and interact with data.

- **Use Cases**: Personal apps, business applications, data dashboards, and interactive forms.

Quick Feature Overview:

Feature	Description
Drag-and-Drop UI	Create mobile apps without coding
AI-Powered Templates	Automatically generate layouts and data handling
Integrations	Sync with data sources like Google Sheets, Airtable

Example Use Case:

- Create an AI-powered **feedback system** where users submit responses via forms, and the app provides automated summaries or insights.

Bubble

- **Purpose**: Bubble is a comprehensive platform for building web applications without writing traditional code. It provides a visual interface to design, manage databases, and deploy web applications.

- **AI Features**: Bubble integrates AI tools like **OpenAI**, allowing developers to add machine learning models, natural language processing (NLP) capabilities, and automated workflows without coding.

- **Use Cases**: Marketplaces, e-commerce sites, social networks, and internal tools with AI functionalities like chatbots or recommendations.

Quick Feature Overview:

Feature	Description
Full Web App Builder	Visual interface for building dynamic web apps
API Integrations	Easily connect with external AI services (e.g., OpenAI, Google Cloud AI)
Real-time Database	Manage data dynamically in real-time

Example Use Case:

- Build a **customer service chatbot** that automates responses and provides recommendations based on user queries, powered by GPT-3 or GPT-4.

---

n8n

- **Purpose**: n8n is an open-source workflow automation platform that allows users to create complex workflows connecting multiple applications, APIs, and services, with minimal coding.

- **AI Features**: n8n integrates with AI services like **OpenAI** and **Google AI**, enabling users to automate tasks like data analysis, content generation, and decision-making.

- **Use Cases**: Automated email campaigns, AI-driven data processing, customer support automation, and AI-driven workflow optimization.

Quick Feature Overview:

Feature	Description
Workflow Automation	Automate repetitive tasks using visual flows
AI Integrations	Use AI services (e.g., OpenAI, Google AI) to enrich workflows
API Connectivity	Integrate various tools to trigger AI-based actions

Example Use Case:

- Set up an automated **email summarization** system where n8n pulls in emails, generates summaries using OpenAI, and sends them out as daily reports.

DeepAgent

- **Purpose**: DeepAgent is a low-code platform focused on creating intelligent applications by integrating deep learning models and AI algorithms.

- **AI Features**: DeepAgent simplifies AI application development with pre-built machine learning models that can be customized for specific tasks. It also offers natural language interfaces and predictive analytics.

- **Use Cases**: Predictive maintenance, AI-powered recommendation engines, business intelligence dashboards.

Quick Feature Overview:

Feature	Description
Pre-built AI Models	Utilize deep learning models for prediction and recommendation
Customization	Customize AI algorithms based on specific use cases
Data Integration	Integrate with data sources to apply AI insights

Example Use Case:

- Build a **predictive analytics tool** for forecasting sales trends based on historical data and AI-driven insights.

8.2 Building Dashboards, Forms, Internal Tools

Creating Dashboards with No-Code/Low-Code Tools

Building data-driven dashboards is one of the most common use cases for no-code and low-code AI platforms. These dashboards allow users to visualize key performance metrics, track progress, and gain insights from data — all without writing code.

Using Glide for Dashboards:

- Glide allows users to easily connect to Google Sheets or Airtable to create real-time dashboards. By using Glide's built-in data processing and visualization features, you can create a dashboard that updates automatically as data changes.

Example Dashboards:

- **Sales Dashboard**: Track sales performance, revenue, and customer interactions, with AI-powered insights into trends or opportunities.

- **Project Management Dashboard**: Visualize team progress, task completion, and deadlines, with AI recommendations for resource allocation.

Using Bubble for Dashboards:

- Bubble allows for more advanced dashboard features, including integration with external data sources (such as APIs) and powerful database management tools. You can display data in graphs, tables, and other visual formats.

Creating Forms with AI Integration

Forms are essential for gathering user input, conducting surveys, or processing data. Many no-code/low-code tools provide easy ways to create forms that integrate directly with AI models to enhance functionality.

Using Glide for Forms:

- Glide allows you to create customizable forms that can automatically capture user data and feed it into a connected database. These forms can trigger AI-powered actions, such as data classification or content generation, once the form is submitted.

Example Use Case:

- **Lead Generation Form**: Capture user details (name, email, preferences) and use AI to generate a personalized email response or content recommendation.

Using n8n for Forms:

- n8n enables users to create automated workflows that are triggered by form submissions. This allows for more complex actions, such as sending notifications, storing data, or initiating AI-based analysis.

Creating Internal Tools with Low-Code Platforms

Internal tools, such as employee dashboards, workflow trackers, and admin panels, are often built on no-code and low-code platforms for their speed and flexibility.

Using Bubble for Internal Tools:

- Build sophisticated internal tools, such as inventory management systems, CRM tools, or team collaboration dashboards, all without the need for extensive programming.

Using DeepAgent for Internal AI Tools:

- Use DeepAgent's low-code environment to quickly prototype AI-driven internal tools for predictive maintenance, employee performance tracking, or decision support systems.

Key Takeaways:

- **No-code and low-code tools** are revolutionizing the way AI-powered applications are created, allowing anyone (regardless of technical expertise) to build functional apps with integrated AI features.

- **Glide**, **Bubble**, **n8n**, and **DeepAgent** are leading platforms that provide simple interfaces for developing applications such as dashboards, forms, and internal tools with AI capabilities.

- **Dashboards** and **forms** are key components of many AI-driven applications, enabling users to easily collect, display, and analyze data.

- These platforms provide a fast, flexible way to build AI-powered solutions that integrate with existing workflows, streamlining tasks like data processing, decision-making, and automation.

8.3 Tool Comparison Table: No-Code Builders

In this section, we compare the major **no-code** and **low-code** platforms mentioned in the previous sections. This table will help you understand the strengths and limitations of each tool, providing a clear view of when and why you should use each one for your AI-powered projects.

Tool	Key Features	Best For	AI Integration	Pricing Model
Glide	Mobile apps from Google Sheets or Excel, drag-and-drop interface	Personal apps, small businesses, customer feedback	AI templates for layout and data processing	Freemium, subscription-based
Bubble	Web app builder, visual interface, full database integration	Web apps, marketplaces, internal tools	Integrates with OpenAI and Google Cloud AI	Freemium, subscription-based
n8n	Workflow automation, open-source, API integrations	Automating tasks, creating custom workflows	Integrates with OpenAI, Google AI, and other APIs	Open-source (Free), Premium features available
DeepAgent	AI-focused low-code platform, pre-built machine learning models	Predictive analytics, AI-powered tools	Pre-built AI models for various use cases	Subscription-based

Summary of Use Cases:

- **Glide**: Best for creating simple, data-driven mobile applications without programming knowledge.

- **Bubble**: Ideal for building sophisticated web applications that require custom workflows and AI integration.

- **n8n**: Perfect for automating tasks, integrating different services, and creating personalized workflows with AI.

- **DeepAgent**: Great for developing AI-powered applications that require deep learning models with minimal coding.

8.4 Common Pitfalls & Best Practices

In this section, we will explore common mistakes that users make when building AI-powered applications with no-code and low-code tools, and provide best practices to help you avoid these pitfalls and make the most of the tools available.

Common Pitfalls

Pitfall	Explanation
1. Overlooking Scalability	No-code and low-code platforms are great for rapid prototyping, but they may not scale well for larger applications. Be mindful of limitations when building long-term projects.
2. Ignoring Data Security and Privacy	Many no-code platforms do not provide built-in security features. It's crucial to consider

	how your data is handled, especially when dealing with sensitive or personal information.
3. Underestimating Maintenance	Even with low-code tools, applications require maintenance. Regular updates, bug fixes, and monitoring are necessary to keep apps running smoothly.
4. Choosing the Wrong Tool for the Job	Not every no-code tool is suited for every project. Some platforms work better for apps, others for automation or workflows. Choose the right tool based on your needs.
5. Overcomplicating Workflows	It can be tempting to create highly complex workflows in no-code platforms. Keep things simple and modular to avoid confusion and issues with performance.
6. Lack of Customization	While no-code tools are easy to use, they can sometimes limit customization. Understand the constraints of your platform and know when it's better to build custom solutions.

Best Practices

Best Practice	Explanation
1. Plan Before You Build	Before diving into the tool, spend time planning the structure of your app or workflow. Know what you want to achieve and break the project into smaller, manageable pieces.
2. Test Early and Often	Test your applications at every stage of development. Early testing helps identify issues quickly and ensures the tool works as expected when scaling up.
3. Keep It Simple	Don't over-engineer your project. The beauty of no-code tools is simplicity. Avoid excessive complexity in workflows and keep user interfaces intuitive.
4. Ensure Data Privacy and Compliance	Always ensure that the platform you are using complies with data privacy regulations (e.g., GDPR) if you handle sensitive information.
5. Leverage Community and Resources	Utilize community forums, documentation, and tutorials. Many no-code platforms offer robust support to help solve issues and maximize efficiency.

6. Monitor and Update Regularly	After deploying, ensure you monitor the application's performance and user feedback. Regular updates and adjustments are vital to keep everything working smoothly.

Common Pitfalls & Best Practices for Specific Platforms

Platform	Pitfalls	Best Practices
Glide	Limited customization options, complex data handling	Use templates wisely, keep data structure simple and organized
Bubble	Performance issues with complex workflows	Optimize workflows and database queries, avoid redundant processes
n8n	Limited out-of-the-box integrations for certain tools	Extend functionality using custom APIs or community-built nodes
DeepAgent	May not support all AI use cases without advanced configurations	Stick to predefined AI models for ease of use, leverage documentation

Key Takeaways

- **Avoid Pitfall 1**: Be cautious of scalability when designing large applications.

- **Practice Best Practice 2**: Test frequently and iteratively.

- **Leverage the right tools for specific use cases**: Use each platform's strengths to your advantage, ensuring they match your project requirements.

Chapter 9: Building with LangChain, RAG, and Agents

LangChain and Retrieval-Augmented Generation (RAG) are at the heart of advanced AI applications, enabling contextual memory, dynamic tool use, and domain-specific knowledge retrieval. This chapter explores how to build intelligent agents, integrate memory, use actions, and harness the power of embeddings and vector databases.

9.1 Agents, Memory, Actions: LangChain, LlamaIndex

Key Concepts

Term	Definition
Agent	An AI that can take actions, use tools, and make decisions in a chain.
Memory	Mechanism for storing and recalling past interactions or information.
Tool Use	Ability of an agent to call APIs, databases, or functions dynamically.

LangChain	A Python framework for building LLM-powered apps using composable modules.
LlamaIndex	A framework to connect LLMs with external data via indexing & retrieval.

Flowchart: Basic Agent Architecture

User Input

   |

   v

LangChain Agent

   |

   |---> Memory (store/retrieve past context)

   |---> Tools (API, function, DB access)

   |

   v

LLM Response

Step-by-Step: Building a Simple LangChain Agent

Install LangChain and OpenAI (or any supported LLM)

```
pip install langchain openai
```

1. **Set up the environment and API key**

```
import os

os.environ["OPENAI_API_KEY"] = "your-key"
```

2. **Create a tool (e.g., calculator)**

```
from langchain.agents import Tool


def add_numbers(x, y):

    return x + y


tools = [Tool(name="Add", func=add_numbers, description="Adds two numbers.")]
```

3. **Build an agent with memory and tools**

```
from langchain.agents import initialize_agent

from langchain.memory import ConversationBufferMemory

from langchain.chat_models import ChatOpenAI


memory = ConversationBufferMemory()

llm = ChatOpenAI(temperature=0)
```

```
agent = initialize_agent(tools, llm, memory=memory, verbose=True)
```

4. **Run the agent**

```
agent.run("What is 2 + 5?")
```

LlamaIndex: Index External Data

- Use LlamaIndex to load data from PDF, Notion, or MySQL.

- Build a vector index for RAG workflows.

```
from llama_index import SimpleDirectoryReader, GPTVectorStoreIndex


documents = SimpleDirectoryReader("data/").load_data()

index = GPTVectorStoreIndex.from_documents(documents)

query_engine = index.as_query_engine()

response = query_engine.query("What is this document about?")

print(response)
```

9.2 Vector Databases, Embeddings, and Custom Search

Key Concepts Table

Concept	Description
Embedding	Numerical representation of text capturing semantic meaning.
Vector Database	Stores and retrieves vectors using similarity search.
FAISS	Facebook's open-source library for efficient vector similarity search.
RAG	Combines retrieval from vector DBs with LLM generation.

Flowchart: Retrieval-Augmented Generation (RAG)

User Query

|

v

Convert to Embedding

|

v

Search Vector DB

|

v

Retrieve Relevant Context

|

v

Feed Context + Query to LLM

|

v

Final Answer Generated

Step-by-Step: Build RAG with FAISS

Install FAISS and Transformers

pip install faiss-cpu sentence-transformers

1. **Generate Embeddings**

```
from sentence_transformers import SentenceTransformer

model = SentenceTransformer('all-MiniLM-L6-v2')
```

```
texts = ["AI is powerful", "LangChain enables agents"]

vectors = model.encode(texts)
```

2. **Create Vector Index with FAISS**

```
import faiss

import numpy as np


index = faiss.IndexFlatL2(384)

index.add(np.array(vectors))
```

3. **Search with a New Query**

```
query = "What can agents do?"

query_vector = model.encode([query])

D, I = index.search(np.array(query_vector), k=1)

print("Most similar text:", texts[I[0][0]])
```

Tool Comparison Table: Vector Databases

Tool	Type	Best For	Pros	Cons
FAISS	Local	Prototyping, speed	Lightweight, fast	No built-in persistence

ChromaDB	Local/Cloud	Docs, apps	Python native, simple setup	Still maturing
Weaviate	Cloud/API	Scalable search apps	GraphQL API, hybrid search	Heavier setup
Pinecone	Cloud	Production deployments	Auto-scaling, real-time	Paid beyond free tier

Key Takeaways

- Use LangChain to build agents that interact with tools and retain memory.

- Integrate vector databases for context-aware generation (RAG).

- LlamaIndex simplifies connecting external data to LLMs.

9.3 Deployment: Vercel, Streamlit, Docker

Tool Comparison Table: Deployment Options

Tool	Best For	Pros	Cons
Streamlit	Rapid UI prototyping	Python-native, easy UI	Less control over frontend
Vercel	Hosting web UIs (Next.js, etc)	Scalable, free tier, CI/CD	JavaScript-focused
Docker	Flexible, portable containers	Full environment control	Requires DevOps knowledge

Step-by-Step: Deploy a LangChain App with Streamlit

Install Streamlit

pip install streamlit

1. **Create a LangChain app file:** app.py

import streamlit as st

from langchain.llms import OpenAI

```python
llm = OpenAI(temperature=0.7)

st.title("Simple LangChain Q&A")

question = st.text_input("Ask me anything")

if question:

    response = llm(question)

    st.write(response)
```

2. **Run the app locally**

   ```
   streamlit run app.py
   ```

3. **Deploy to Streamlit Cloud**

   - Push your code to GitHub.

   - Go to https://share.streamlit.io, log in, and connect the repo.

   - It will auto-deploy and give you a public link.

Docker Deployment Example

Create Dockerfile

```
FROM python:3.10

WORKDIR /app

COPY . /app
```

RUN pip install -r requirements.txt

CMD ["streamlit", "run", "app.py", "--server.port=8501", "--server.enableCORS=false"]

1. **Build and run the Docker container**

```
docker build -t langchain-app .
```

docker run -p 8501:8501 langchain-app

2. **Your app runs at:** http://localhost:8501

9.4 Mini Case Study: Q&A App with LangChain

Project Title: *Ask Your Docs* – A Q&A App Using LangChain + LlamaIndex

---

Tech Stack

- LangChain for orchestration

- LlamaIndex for indexing and retrieval

- Streamlit for UI

- FAISS or Chroma for local vector storage

App Workflow Diagram

User Uploads Document

   |

   v

LlamaIndex Creates Vector Index

   |

   v

User Asks Question

   |

   v

Relevant Context Retrieved from Index

   |

   v

LangChain Agent Generates Answer

   |

   v

Display Answer to User

Code Sketch

```python
import streamlit as st
```

```python
from llama_index import SimpleDirectoryReader, GPTVectorStoreIndex


# Step 1: Upload file

st.title("Ask Your Docs")

uploaded_file = st.file_uploader("Upload a document", type=["pdf", "txt"])

if uploaded_file:

    with open(f"data/{uploaded_file.name}", "wb") as f:

        f.write(uploaded_file.read())


    # Step 2: Build Index

    docs = SimpleDirectoryReader("data/").load_data()

    index = GPTVectorStoreIndex.from_documents(docs)

    query_engine = index.as_query_engine()


    # Step 3: Ask questions

    question = st.text_input("Ask a question about your document")

    if question:

        response = query_engine.query(question)

        st.write("Answer:", response)
```

Use Case Impact

- **Education**: Students upload lecture notes, ask for summaries or explanations.

- **Law**: Lawyers query legal documents or contracts.

- **Healthcare**: Doctors access medical guidelines or patient history instantly.

Key Takeaways

- Streamlit is ideal for quick UI deployment of LangChain apps.

- Docker ensures environment consistency for any host.

- Combining LlamaIndex + LangChain allows real-time document Q&A with high relevance.

9.5 Common Pitfalls & Best Practices

Common Pitfalls

Pitfall	Description	How to Avoid
Overloading the Agent	Giving too many tools or unclear instructions to the agent can lead to failure in task completion.	Start with one or two tools, clearly define roles and outputs.

Lack of Error Handling	Ignoring exceptions during API calls or vector search results in silent failures.	Use try-except blocks and meaningful user feedback.
Poor Indexing Strategy	Indexing documents without chunking or metadata causes irrelevant results.	Use chunking + metadata filtering (e.g., section titles, tags).
Latency Issues	Query time increases with large datasets or remote vector stores.	Use local vector DBs (like Chroma or FAISS), batch inference if needed.
Generic Prompts	Weak or vague prompts produce inaccurate responses.	Use prompt templates with structure and examples.

Best Practices

Tip	Description
Modular Design	Break app logic into components (ingestion, retrieval, UI, etc.).
Prompt Templates	Create reusable and testable prompt structures.

Tool Isolation	Test each tool (agent, retriever, LLM) in isolation before integration.
User Feedback Loops	Allow users to rate outputs to improve prompt quality over time.
Local Dev First	Build and test locally before deploying to cloud platforms.
Security First	Sanitize user inputs, especially when using dynamic prompts or APIs.

Project Recap: Build an AI-Powered SaaS App with or without Code

Key Components

Component	Description	Tools
Frontend	User interface for uploads and queries	Streamlit / Bubble / Webflow
Backend	Handles document ingestion, vector search, AI response	LangChain / LlamaIndex / Python

Vector Store	Stores document embeddings	Chroma / FAISS / Pinecone
Deployment	Host the application	Streamlit Cloud / Vercel / Docker

Flowchart: SaaS Q&A App Lifecycle

User Signup/Login

  |

  v

Upload Document --> Chunk + Embed --> Store in Vector DB

  |

  v

Enter Query --> Retrieve Context --> Run LLM Prompt --> Show Result

Bonus: No-Code Approach

Step	Tool	Action
UI	Glide / Softr	Create form for file upload

Workflow	Make / n8n	Automate upload → vector embed → GPT prompt
AI	DeepAgent	No-code orchestration of AI logic
Output	Email / App UI	Send results to user or show in-app

Success Criteria

- User uploads a file and receives context-aware answers.

- System can scale from one user to thousands.

- Prompt performance improves via feedback loops.

Part IV: Creating with Art, Music, and Video

Chapter 10: AI Image Generation

10.1 Midjourney, DALL·E, Stable Diffusion

Introduction

Generative AI models for visual creation have revolutionized how we design, illustrate, and imagine visuals. This section introduces the leading tools in AI image generation, their use cases, and how to apply them effectively for both artistic and practical projects.

Concept Explanation

Generative AI image tools convert text-based descriptions (prompts) into high-quality visuals using trained deep learning models. Each tool has a unique approach:

Tool	Model Type	Access Method	Ideal Use Case
Midjourney	Diffusion (cloud)	Discord-based bot	Artistic and stylized images
DALL·E	Transformer-based	Web, API (OpenAI)	General-purpose image gen
Stable Diffusion	Diffusion (open-source)	Local/cloud apps	Custom, fine-tuned visuals

Tool Snapshot Table

Tool	Prompt Control	Editing Features	Open Source	API Available
Midjourney	High (via styles)	No (no inpainting)	No	No
DALL·E 3	Moderate	Yes (inpainting)	No	Yes (OpenAI)
Stable Diffusion	Very High	Yes (full control)	Yes	Via providers

Step-by-Step Guide: Generating with DALL·E (OpenAI)

1. Sign in at platform.openai.com

2. Navigate to **DALL·E** image generation section.

3. Enter your prompt, such as:

   "A futuristic city at night in the style of cyberpunk, neon colors"

4. Review generated outputs.

5. Click on an image to edit or use the inpainting tool.

Flowchart: Prompt to Image Pipeline

Start

|

v

Input Text Prompt

|

v

Text is Tokenized and Interpreted by Model

|

v

Latent Image Representation is Generated

|

v

Image is Rendered via Diffusion Process

|

v

Output Preview Displayed

Tip:

Be specific in your prompt. Include style, color, subject, and emotion for best results.

10.2 Style Control, Inpainting, Edits

Concept Explanation

Advanced control features allow users to refine images with precision. Key methods include:

- **Style Control**: Adjust visual output by using descriptive modifiers (e.g., "oil painting," "vintage photo").

- **Inpainting**: Edit specific parts of an image (available in DALL·E and SD-based tools).

- **Prompt Weighting**: Emphasize or de-emphasize elements using parentheses or tokens (Stable Diffusion).

- **Negative Prompts**: Specify what *not* to include in the image.

Table: Prompt Modifiers & Their Effects

Modifier Example	Effect
"in the style of Van Gogh"	Impressionist painting look
"low poly, 3D render"	Geometric digital art
"high contrast, dark tones"	Moodier, cinematic appearance
"--no text, --no watermark"	Removes unwanted elements (SD only)

Common Use Cases

Use Case	Tool	Notes
Product Mockups	DALL·E, SD	Combine with inpainting
Album Covers	Midjourney	Style-rich, vibrant output
Book Illustrations	SD, Midjourney	Fine-tuned control needed

Prompt Engineering Tips

- Use the format:

  "Subject, Style, Lighting, Composition, Camera Lens, Environment"

- Example:

  "A portrait of a robot barista, cyberpunk style, soft lighting, 35mm lens, in a neon café"

10.3 Mini Case Study: AI in Advertising Design

Scenario: Ad Agency Integrates AI for Rapid Visual Concepts

Background:

A mid-sized creative agency, *Nova AdWorks*, faced rising client demands for rapid visual mockups during pitch presentations. Traditional workflows using graphic designers alone took 2–3 days to create 3 concept drafts.

AI Integration:

The agency introduced **Midjourney** and **Stable Diffusion** into its creative workflow.
Copywriters and strategists were trained to use prompt templates to generate initial visuals.

Workflow Flowchart: Human-AI Collaborative Design

Client Brief

|

v

Strategist Writes Prompt

|

v

Image Generated via Midjourney/SD

|

v

Design Team Reviews & Refines

|

v

Client Presentation

Key Outcomes

Metric	Before AI	After AI Integration
Time to First Draft	2–3 days	1–2 hours
Number of Concepts per Pitch	3	6–8
Client Approval Rate	60% on first try	85% on first try
Designer Workload	High	Shifted to refinement

Benefits Noted by the Agency

- **Speed**: Faster iteration cycles enabled more agile client feedback.

- **Creativity**: AI-generated ideas inspired designers to explore new directions.

- **Client Engagement**: Clients were impressed by the novelty and customizability.

Common Prompts Used

"A minimalistic tech product banner, white background, floating elements, futuristic typeface"
"A surreal advertisement featuring coffee and clouds, dreamy atmosphere, photo-realistic"

Tip:

AI doesn't replace human designers—it enhances brainstorming and unlocks speed.

10.4 Prompt Poster (Printable via QR)

As per your previous direction to omit QR code generation, this section will refer to the **Prompt Poster** as a downloadable, text-only companion file. Here's how the content would be described:

Text-Based Prompt Poster: Visual Creation Prompts

A printable sheet of structured, modular prompt templates for generating stunning images with any GenAI tool.

Section Highlights:

Prompt Type	Structure Template Example
Product Ad	"A [product] on a [background], in the style of [style], [lighting]"
Portrait	"A portrait of a [subject], [emotion], [style], [camera type]"
Scene Design	"A [place or setting], [time of day], [mood], in [art style]"

10.5 Common Pitfalls & Best Practices

Table: Do's and Don'ts for AI Image Generation

Do	Don't
Use clear, descriptive prompts with specific keywords	Use vague or generic phrases like "make it look good"
Experiment with styles, lighting, and composition terms	Expect perfect results with a single prompt
Refine outputs through iterations and prompt tweaking	Rely on one model output as final artwork
Check license/usage rights of AI-generated images	Assume all generated art is commercially safe
Use post-processing tools for polish and enhancement	Use raw outputs without human review or curation
Align style and format with brand guidelines	Overuse surreal or inconsistent styles in professional work

Important Tips:

- **Tip:** Always define the *subject, environment, style, and mood* in your prompt for best results.

- **Note:** Some tools like Midjourney do not allow NSFW content; review their terms carefully.

- **Important:** Even high-quality images can carry biases—review outputs critically for fairness and inclusivity.

Best Practice Flowchart: Prompt Development Loop

Initial Prompt

|

v

Generate Image

|

v

Evaluate Output (Clarity, Relevance, Style)

|

+--> If Unsatisfactory --> Refine Prompt & Repeat

|

v

Finalize & Use (Post-process if needed)

Pro-Level Prompting Formula (Text)

"[Subject] in [Style], using [Lighting] with [Composition] — [Resolution or aspect ratio]"

Example:

"A futuristic city skyline at night in the style of cyberpunk, neon lighting, isometric perspective — 16:9"

Chapter 11: Audio & Music Creation

Introduction

The convergence of generative AI with sound has opened new creative dimensions in music composition, voice synthesis, and audio storytelling. This chapter explores tools and workflows that allow users—regardless of musical or technical background—to create compelling audio and voice content.

11.1 Tools: Aiva, Boomy, Soundraw, ElevenLabs

Concept Overview

Generative AI tools for audio fall into three main categories:

- **AI Music Composition:** Automates melody, harmony, and instrumental arrangements.

- **Voice Synthesis:** Produces lifelike speech, accents, and emotional tones.

- **Soundtrack & Voiceover Tools:** For commercial, entertainment, and educational uses.

Tool Comparison Table:

Tool	Purpose	Strength	Limitation
Aiva	AI music composition	Classical, cinematic scoring	Less control over modern genres

Boomy	Auto-music generation	Instant tracks, beginner-friendly	Simpler compositions
Soundraw	Music for content creators	Genre-specific generation	Licensing needed for monetization
ElevenLabs	Voice synthesis	Realistic voice cloning	Limited cloning without a plan

Flowchart: AI Music Generation Workflow

Start

|

v

Select Tool (Aiva / Boomy / Soundraw)

|

v

Choose Style / Mood / Genre

|

v

Generate & Edit Track

|

v

Export Audio / Integrate into Project

11.2 Voice Cloning, Dubbing, Audiobooks

Concept Overview

Voice cloning and dubbing technologies allow creators to personalize audio content, localize media, and produce narration with expressive tone and nuance.

Key Capabilities:

- **Voice Cloning:** Replicates a human voice using AI from minimal samples

- **AI Dubbing:** Translates and syncs voices across languages

- **Audiobooks:** Auto-narrates long-form content in natural speech

---

Step-by-Step Guide: AI Voice Generation with ElevenLabs

1. Sign up at ElevenLabs.io

2. Record a 60-second voice sample

3. Upload your script or text

4. Generate the audio

5. Export as MP3 or integrate with a video editor

Flowchart: Audiobook Narration Workflow

Start

|

v

Prepare Text or eBook File

|

v

Clone or Choose Voice Model

|

v

Adjust Voice Settings (Pitch, Speed, Emotion)

|

v

Generate Narration

|

v

Export Audio or Integrate with Media

Prompt Example: Narration via API (ElevenLabs)

```python
import requests


API_KEY = 'your_api_key'

voice_id = 'your_voice_id'

text = "Welcome to the future of voice generation."


response = requests.post(

    f'https://api.elevenlabs.io/v1/text-to-speech/{voice_id}',

    headers={'xi-api-key': API_KEY},

    json={'text': text, 'voice_settings': {'stability': 0.7, 'similarity_boost': 0.85}}

)


with open('narration.mp3', 'wb') as f:

    f.write(response.content)
```

Best Practices Table

Do	Don't
Get consent for voice cloning	Clone voices without permission
Use tools for ethical storytelling	Mislead audiences with fake voiceovers
Test voices for clarity and tone	Rely on default settings blindly

Callouts

- **Important:** Check legal and ethical use of cloned voices, especially in commercial projects.

- **Tip:** Use different voice profiles for character-driven stories or multi-speaker content.

- **Note:** Some tools offer multilingual dubbing for broader accessibility.

11.3 Mini Case Study: AI in Film Sound Design

Project Title:

"Silent Signals": Enhancing Indie Sci-Fi Film Soundscapes with AI Tools

Background:

An independent filmmaker working on a low-budget science fiction film needed high-quality ambient sound effects and futuristic audio cues. Due to financial constraints, they couldn't hire a full sound design team.

Solution:

The filmmaker integrated AI sound design tools such as **Soundraw** for cinematic background music and **ElevenLabs** for synthetic voiceovers. They also used open-source models to generate environmental effects like engine hums, atmospheric noise, and alien signals.

Workflow:

1. **Scene Breakdown**

   Identified key moments requiring audio enhancements (spacewalk, intercom dialogue, ship launch).

2. **Sound Generation with AI**

   - Used **Soundraw** to generate ambient loops based on mood (tense, eerie, calm).

   - Leveraged **Riffusion** to experiment with synthetic sci-fi sound textures.

3. **Voiceover Dubbing with ElevenLabs**

   - Cloned actor voices for robotic intercoms.

   - Added accent-modified voices for alien transmissions.

4. **Audio Integration**

   - Synced AI-generated tracks using DaVinci Resolve.

   - Applied dynamic range compression to balance AI audio with recorded vocals.

Outcome:

The AI-enhanced audio made the film more immersive, saved over 80% in sound production costs, and helped the filmmaker win accolades at indie film festivals for innovation in sound design.

11.4 Tool Comparison Table: Audio & Sound Design Tools

Tool	Function	Best Use Case	Limitations
Aiva	Music composition	Cinematic or emotional background scores	Limited beat-driven or pop genres
Boomy	Instant music generation	Quick tracks for casual videos	Less control over individual tracks
Soundraw	Genre-specific music loops	Vlogs, ads, indie films	Requires paid license for commercial
ElevenLabs	Text-to-speech, voice cloning	Narration, dubbing, voice interfaces	Cloning limits on free accounts
Riffusion	Real-time music from spectrograms	Experimental sound effects	Experimental, low control

Descript Overdub	Voiceover editing & cloning	Podcast, YouTube narration	Quality depends on training data
Voice.ai	Real-time voice changing	Gaming, streaming, character voices	Latency and authenticity issues

Callouts

- **Tip:** Combine multiple tools for layered audio complexity (e.g., voice + ambiance + music).

- **Note:** Always check licensing terms when publishing audio commercially.

- **Important:** Use spatial audio simulation plugins for VR and immersive media projects.

11.5 Common Pitfalls & Best Practices

Creating audio and music with AI can significantly speed up production, but there are key mistakes to avoid and best practices to adopt.

Do vs Don't Table

Do	Don't
Test multiple AI tools to compare quality and features	Settle on the first tool you try
Check copyright and usage licenses before publishing	Assume all AI-generated audio is royalty-free
Fine-tune AI voice generation with proper training data	Use poor-quality samples or skip voice customization
Combine AI-generated elements with human input for best results	Rely solely on AI for emotion-driven or nuanced performances
Use editing tools to smooth transitions and sync with visuals	Let AI audio run without post-production cleanup
Maintain consistent volume levels and audio dynamics across tracks	Ignore mastering steps—this creates uneven listening experiences
Backup and document versions of generated files	Forget to save intermediate files or original AI settings

Best Practices

- **Structure First:** Outline your audio needs by scene, mood, or message before generating content.

- **Prompt Carefully:** Be specific with mood, genre, tempo, and instruments (e.g., "Slow ambient music with synth pads and piano").

- **Layer for Depth:** Combine ambient textures, sound effects, and music for a rich soundscape.

- **Use High-Quality Export Settings:** Choose lossless formats (like WAV) when possible, especially for professional use.

- **Collaborate with Sound Engineers:** Use AI for draft creation, but let professionals refine final output when budget allows.

Tip:

Use AI tools as co-creators, not replacements — they're most powerful when integrated thoughtfully with your creative process.

Chapter 12: Video Creation with AI

12.1 RunwayML, Synthesia, HeyGen, Pictory

Generative AI tools for video creation have transformed the way content is produced, from editing to animation. In this section, we'll explore some of the most popular platforms for AI-driven video production.

RunwayML

- **Overview:** RunwayML provides an intuitive platform for creators to harness AI in video editing, including tools for object detection, video inpainting, and real-time collaboration.

- **Key Features:**

    - AI-assisted video editing tools

    - Real-time video generation

    - Style transfer for visual effects

    - Cross-platform compatibility

- **Best For:** Content creators, marketers, and video editors looking to integrate AI in video production.

Synthesia

- **Overview:** Synthesia specializes in AI video synthesis, enabling users to create talking-head videos with AI-generated avatars. It's widely used for corporate training, e-learning, and marketing.

- **Key Features:**

  - Text-to-speech in multiple languages

  - Avatar creation and customization

  - Integration with existing media libraries

- **Best For:** Enterprises, marketing teams, and educational content creators.

HeyGen

- **Overview:** HeyGen offers AI tools to generate talking avatars for marketing, education, and more. It can generate videos from text and produce realistic avatars for user interaction.

- **Key Features:**

  - Realistic avatar generation

  - Multi-language support

  - Real-time video synthesis from text

- **Best For:** Social media content creators, educators, and businesses.

Pictory

- **Overview:** Pictory is an AI tool that helps creators transform scripts or articles into engaging videos. It's particularly useful for generating short-form content for platforms like TikTok and Instagram.

- **Key Features:**

  - Convert text articles into video summaries

  - Stock video and image integration

  - Easy export to social media formats

- **Best For:** Bloggers, YouTubers, and social media marketers.

12.2 Reels, Ads, Avatars, Lip Sync & Deepfakes

AI has revolutionized video content production for social media, advertising, and even entertainment. Understanding how these tools can be applied creatively is essential for marketers, content creators, and developers.

Reels & Short-Form Video

- **AI in Short Videos:** Tools like Pictory and RunwayML are excellent for creating short-form video content (e.g., Instagram Reels, TikTok, YouTube Shorts). AI can automate video editing, add effects, and suggest cuts to fit the time constraints of these platforms.

- **Best Practices:** Use AI to automate repetitive editing tasks and enhance creative flow, but always review final output for pacing, engagement, and quality.

AI in Ads Creation

- **AI-Generated Ad Videos:** Generative tools can help create professional ad videos quickly by using templates, dynamic text generation, and even creating personalized avatars for commercials. Platforms like Synthesia can produce localized, multilingual ads.

- **Best Practices:** Personalize ads based on viewer data, utilize AI-generated avatars for relatable, diverse characters, and ensure your call-to-action is clear and strong.

Avatars and Virtual Influencers

- **AI-Generated Avatars:** With tools like HeyGen and Synthesia, you can create digital avatars to represent a brand or persona in videos. These avatars can speak directly to audiences, promoting a personalized and engaging experience.

- **Best Practices:** Make sure the avatars feel authentic and relatable, especially in influencer marketing. The key is balancing technology and human connection.

Lip Sync & Deepfakes

- **AI-Powered Lip Sync:** Tools like Synthesia allow users to create realistic lip-syncing videos. These are often used in education, entertainment, or for creating virtual influencers.

- **Deepfakes:** AI-generated deepfakes allow for highly realistic video manipulations, like changing a person's face or voice. While this can be used creatively, it must be handled with care to avoid ethical and legal concerns.

- **Best Practices:**

  - **Ethical Use:** Always disclose the use of deepfake technology, especially for advertisements or entertainment.

  - **Verification:** Ensure all AI-generated content aligns with your brand's ethical guidelines.

12.3 Mini Case Study: Corporate AI Training Videos

Background:

A global technology company needed a scalable solution for training its employees across various departments. Traditional training methods (in-person sessions and static e-learning modules) were costly and time-consuming. The company decided to leverage AI video generation tools to create engaging, interactive training videos that could be customized and localized for different regions.

The Solution:

The company used **Synthesia** and **RunwayML** to create a series of training videos. Here's how they approached the project:

1. **Avatar Creation:**

   o Using **Synthesia**, they generated digital avatars of trainers speaking in multiple languages. These avatars were tailored to appear professional and relatable to different employee demographics.

2. **Video Scripting and Content Generation:**

   o The scripts were created using AI-assisted tools like **GPT-4** for natural language generation, ensuring that the content was clear, concise, and relevant to the target audience.

3. **Video Editing:**

   o **RunwayML** was used for video editing, including adding dynamic text overlays, transitions, and effects to make the training materials more engaging.

4. **Localization:**

- For regional differences, AI tools were used to create different language versions of the training videos, ensuring that the content could be localized easily without needing to reshoot videos or hire new voice actors.

5. **Distribution:**

   - The final videos were uploaded to the company's internal platform and linked with a **Pictory**-generated summary video, allowing employees to access bite-sized training materials.

Outcome:

- The company saw a **40% increase in employee engagement** due to the high-quality, easily digestible AI-powered training videos.

- Training time was reduced by **60%** since the videos could be used repeatedly across different teams and regions.

- Employees appreciated the convenience and consistency of the content, and the company reduced its training costs significantly.

12.4 Common Pitfalls & Best Practices

Common Pitfalls

Pitfall	Explanation
Over-Reliance on AI for Creativity	AI can speed up content creation, but over-relying on it can lead to bland, generic output. Always add a human touch.
Lack of Personalization	AI-generated avatars and videos can feel impersonal. Personalize content to fit your target audience's needs.
Ignoring Ethical Guidelines	The use of AI in video production, especially with deepfakes, can raise ethical concerns. Always disclose AI-generated content and avoid using it for misleading purposes.
Inadequate Quality Control	AI-generated content still needs human oversight. Always check the final output for quality, accuracy, and consistency.
Underestimating Cultural Sensitivity	AI-generated content should be sensitive to cultural norms. Localization is key to ensuring respect and relevance.

Best Practices

Best Practice	Explanation
Leverage AI for Time-Saving, Not Creativity	Use AI for tasks like video editing, avatar generation, and translation, but maintain creative control.
Ensure Consistency	For brand consistency, ensure AI tools align with your brand's style and message.
Incorporate Human Feedback	Always have a human review the AI-generated content for contextual accuracy and emotional tone.
Test Across Multiple Platforms	AI-generated video may look different across various devices and platforms. Always test before final release.
Maintain Transparency	Be clear with your audience that AI-generated content is used, particularly when using avatars, voiceovers, or deepfakes.

Project Recap: Create a Video, Voiceover, and Poster Using Only AI Tools

Step-by-Step Guide:

1. **Create the Video:**

   - **Tool:** Use **RunwayML** or **Synthesia** to create an AI-powered video. Choose a template, upload your script, and select an avatar or presenter.

   - **Output:** Generate a 1-minute promotional video with dynamic text and effects.

2. **Add a Voiceover:**

   - **Tool:** Use **ElevenLabs** or **Aiva** to generate a voiceover based on your script.

   - **Output:** Create a high-quality voiceover that aligns with the tone of the video.

3. **Design the Poster:**

   - **Tool:** Use **Midjourney** or **Canva** (AI-assisted features) to generate a visually appealing poster.

   - **Output:** Create a poster that encapsulates the theme of your video using AI-generated designs.

Result:

- A seamless promotional content package (video, voiceover, and poster) generated entirely using AI tools, reducing production time and costs.

Part V: Innovation, Monetization, and Ethics

Chapter 13: Innovation & Rapid Prototyping

13.1 Brainstorming, Prototyping, and Mockups

Introduction

Innovation thrives in environments where ideas are allowed to flourish, and **AI tools** can greatly enhance creativity and speed up the process. This chapter focuses on how to use generative AI tools to facilitate brainstorming, rapid prototyping, and creating mockups for your projects.

Brainstorming with AI:

AI-driven brainstorming tools provide **fresh perspectives**, expand your creative horizons, and speed up idea generation.

1. **Mind Mapping:**
   AI can help organize thoughts and ideas quickly. By inputting a central concept, AI tools can suggest related topics, creating a robust idea map.

2. **AI-Driven Idea Generation:**
   Use tools like **ChatGPT** to generate diverse ideas based on a set of inputs (e.g., market trends, user needs). This accelerates ideation without getting stuck in mental blocks.

3. **Collaborative Brainstorming:**
   AI platforms allow multiple users to contribute ideas simultaneously, even across remote teams. Tools like **Miro** and **MURAL** integrate AI for real-time collaboration.

Prototyping with AI:

AI simplifies the process of turning concepts into actionable prototypes.

1. **Rapid Prototyping:**

- Tools like **Figma** leverage AI to assist with design iterations. Figma's auto-layout features, powered by AI, can adjust designs quickly, based on preset rules or user input.

- **RunwayML** and **Adobe Firefly** offer quick design prototypes and iterative changes, especially for projects requiring dynamic visuals.

2. **Mockups:**

- **Uizard**: Generates user interfaces and app mockups automatically from text prompts. Simply describe your app, and Uizard can generate basic designs with suggested layouts.

- **Figma**: In combination with AI plugins, can generate various interface designs, visual styles, and prototypes based on specific inputs (e.g., "Create a social media app UI").

Key Benefits of AI in Prototyping:

- **Speed**: AI tools help you prototype designs faster by suggesting layouts, colors, and content structures.

- **Iterative Design**: AI assists in testing and refining prototypes based on feedback loops.

- **Cost Efficiency**: Reduces reliance on graphic designers or UI/UX experts for initial prototypes, cutting costs.

Best Practices:

Best Practice	Explanation
Define Clear Objectives	Before prototyping, establish clear goals for what you want to achieve with the design.
Leverage AI to Save Time	Use AI for initial brainstorming and mockups, but refine the design with human oversight.
Test Iterations	Continuously iterate with AI, making small tweaks for optimal results.
Ensure Flexibility	Ensure the prototype can be easily modified as you discover new insights.

13.2 Figma, Diagram, UIzard, and Ideation Tools

Introduction

Figma, Diagram, **UIzard**, and other AI-powered ideation tools are game-changers in the rapid prototyping and mockup creation process. In this section, we'll compare some of the most popular tools that harness AI to streamline design workflows.

Figma:

Figma is a collaborative design tool widely used for UI/UX design and prototyping.

- **Key Features:**

  - **Auto Layout**: Automatically adjusts design elements based on content and screen size, helping designers create responsive layouts quickly.

  - **Plugins**: Many AI-powered Figma plugins assist in generating quick mockups, organizing content, and creating visual elements.

  - **Design Systems**: AI tools suggest UI components based on your design style or brand guidelines.

- **Best Use Case**: Ideal for teams working collaboratively on designs, prototyping user interfaces, and iterating quickly with AI-powered suggestions.

Diagram:

Diagram is an AI-powered tool for flowcharting and diagramming complex systems. It's often used for building system architecture, flow diagrams, and decision trees.

- **Key Features:**

  - **AI Layout Optimization**: Diagram uses AI to optimize flowcharts for readability and coherence.

  - **Auto-Generate Diagrams**: Simply describe a process, and **Diagram** will suggest the appropriate flow and structure.

- **Best Use Case**: Perfect for prototyping business workflows, software systems, and decision-making processes.

UIzard:

UIzard is an AI-powered tool for generating **UI mockups** from text prompts. It is designed to assist developers and designers by quickly generating interface designs.

- **Key Features:**

    - **Text to UI**: Input simple text descriptions, such as "Create a mobile banking app," and Ulzard will generate a UI prototype that matches your description.

    - **Customization**: After generating the initial mockup, you can customize it further using drag-and-drop features.

- **Best Use Case**: Ideal for entrepreneurs, startups, or solo developers who need to quickly visualize a UI without deep design knowledge.

Other Ideation Tools:

- **Miro**: A digital whiteboard tool that offers AI-based suggestions for brainstorming, user journey mapping, and agile planning.

- **MURAL**: Another collaborative whiteboarding tool that helps teams brainstorm, plan, and visualize workflows with AI-driven design suggestions.

Tool Comparison Table:

Tool Name	Primary Use	AI Features	Best For
Figma	UI/UX design & prototyping	Auto layout, AI plugins for rapid prototyping	Collaborative UI design teams
Diagram	Flowcharting & diagramming	AI layout optimization, auto-	Process modeling and workflow mapping

		generation of diagrams	
Ulzard	UI mockup generation from text	Text to UI transformation, drag-and-drop editing	Startups, solo developers
Miro	Digital whiteboarding	AI-driven brainstorming and planning templates	Remote team collaboration
MURAL	Visual collaboration & ideation	AI-driven visual suggestions for team workshops	Idea generation and concept development

13.3 From the Expert: AI in UX/UI Design

Introduction

AI's role in UX/UI design is rapidly evolving, and many design experts now view it as a powerful tool that can enhance creativity, streamline workflows, and improve user experiences. As AI continues to grow in sophistication, it's reshaping how designers approach challenges, from creating personalized experiences to refining design systems. To explore this further, we've interviewed several experts in the field, a seasoned UX/UI designer with experience working at top design agencies and leading AI-based design initiatives.

Key Insights from the Expert:

1. **AI as a Design Assistant:**
   According to experts in the field, AI isn't meant to replace designers but to act as a

supportive assistant, automating repetitive tasks and offering creative suggestions. Tools like **Figma** and **Sketch** integrated with AI can provide automatic layout adjustments, suggest color schemes, and generate consistent design elements based on user data. This frees up designers to focus more on strategy and innovation.

2. **Personalization and Dynamic Design:**

   AI is revolutionizing personalization in UX/UI design. By leveraging data and predictive models, AI can tailor designs to the individual user's preferences, behaviors, and needs. For example, AI-powered personalization engines can create dynamic layouts and content that adapt in real-time based on user interaction, offering a more personalized experience.

3. **AI for Prototyping and Testing:**

   Rapid prototyping is one of the most transformative applications of AI in design. Experts are increasingly relying on tools like **Uizard** to quickly generate prototype designs from text descriptions. These AI-driven tools enable rapid experimentation with various layouts, streamlining the early stages of design. Additionally, AI can run tests and simulations on design prototypes, helping designers identify usability issues early in the process.

4. **Ethical Considerations in Design:**

   As AI becomes a key player in UX/UI design, the expert stresses the importance of considering ethical implications. AI tools must be carefully monitored to ensure they promote **inclusive** and **accessible** designs. Designers should remain mindful of biases in AI-generated designs and ensure their tools are used to create equitable user experiences.

5. **The Future of UX/UI Design:**

   Looking ahead, the expert envisions AI playing a significant role in the **creation of fully interactive interfaces**. With advances in voice recognition, gesture control, and adaptive AI, designers will be able to create interfaces that respond intelligently to the user's behavior, improving accessibility and engagement.

Expert's Final Thoughts:

"AI is not a tool to fear—it's a tool to enhance your abilities. The future of UX/UI design is collaborative between human creativity and machine intelligence. Designers who embrace AI will find themselves equipped with powerful new tools that enhance their creativity and speed up the design process."

13.4 Common Pitfalls & Best Practices

Common Pitfalls in AI-Driven UX/UI Design

Pitfall	Explanation
Over-Automation	Relying too heavily on AI for all aspects of the design process can result in designs that lack the unique touch of human creativity. AI-generated designs may sometimes feel sterile or uninspired.
Ignoring User Feedback	While AI tools can create designs based on data, user feedback is crucial for improving usability and ensuring the design meets real-world needs. Without testing, AI-driven designs can fail to meet expectations.
Lack of Inclusivity	AI tools often rely on historical data and patterns, which can inadvertently result in biased or exclusionary designs. It's important

	to ensure that designs are inclusive and cater to a diverse range of users.
Complexity Over Simplicity	AI can create intricate designs, but simple, intuitive designs often provide the best user experience. Overcomplicating designs with too many features or flashy elements can confuse users.
Not Understanding AI Limitations	Designers may expect AI tools to understand the nuances of creative design. However, AI lacks the context, empathy, and human intuition necessary to truly understand emotional or aesthetic aspects of design.

Best Practices for AI-Driven UX/UI Design

Best Practice	Explanation
Collaborate with AI, Don't Rely on It	Use AI tools to assist in tasks like layout generation and prototyping, but always incorporate your own design intuition and creative judgment. AI should complement, not replace, your expertise.
Test, Iterate, and Get Feedback	Regularly test AI-generated designs with real users and gather feedback to refine and improve your designs. Rapid prototyping

	allows for quick iterations, so use this to your advantage.
Focus on User-Centered Design	Even though AI can optimize designs based on data, always prioritize user needs and preferences. Use AI tools to enhance personalization, but ensure that designs remain intuitive and accessible for all users.
Be Mindful of Ethical Considerations	Consider the potential biases that may arise from AI-generated designs. Be proactive in ensuring your designs are inclusive, fair, and accessible to all user groups.
Keep Designs Simple and Functional	Avoid over-complicating your designs with AI-generated elements that are flashy but unnecessary. Simple, clean designs with clear functionality will always provide the best user experience.
Maintain a Balance Between Creativity and Automation	Use AI tools for repetitive or data-driven tasks but retain your creative control over design decisions that involve user emotion, aesthetics, and deeper context.

Chapter 14: Monetizing with Gen AI

14.1 Freelancing, Consulting, Products, Marketplaces

Generative AI is opening up new avenues for monetization, enabling individuals and businesses to generate revenue through a wide range of applications. Whether you're a freelancer, consultant, or business owner, understanding the opportunities available can help you build a profitable venture using AI technologies.

Freelancing with Generative AI

Freelancers are increasingly leveraging AI tools to provide services such as content generation, chatbot creation, and automated workflows. These services can be offered through various platforms such as **Upwork**, **Fiverr**, or **Toptal**, where clients are looking for expertise in AI tools and applications.

Key Freelance Opportunities:

- **Content Creation**: Writing blogs, articles, social media posts, and SEO-optimized content using AI-powered writing tools like **Jasper** or **Copy.ai**.

- **AI-Generated Art**: Using tools like **Midjourney**, **DALL·E**, and **Stable Diffusion** to create AI-generated visual art for clients in design, advertising, and marketing.

- **AI Chatbot Development**: Building custom chatbots and virtual assistants for businesses using platforms like **Rasa**, **ChatGPT**, or **Claude**.

- **AI-driven Web Development**: Automating web design and development tasks using no-code platforms such as **Bubble** and **Webflow**, or by offering specialized development services for AI-driven apps.

Consulting with Generative AI

Consultants can offer valuable advice on how businesses can integrate generative AI into their operations. From strategy development to technical implementation, AI consulting services are in high demand.

Key Consulting Areas:

- **AI Integration**: Helping companies integrate AI into their products, services, and workflows. This can include recommending the right tools, overseeing implementation, and providing training.

- **AI for Marketing**: Advising on how AI can automate marketing campaigns, create personalized customer experiences, and improve ROI.

- **AI for Automation**: Consulting on AI-driven workflow automation, including integrating AI tools like **Zapier**, **n8n**, and **Make** to streamline operations.

Selling Products with Generative AI

Entrepreneurs can create and sell AI-powered products. From software as a service (SaaS) platforms to AI-generated content tools, the possibilities are vast.

Potential Products to Sell:

- **AI Writing Tools**: Develop and sell subscription-based AI writing tools or content generation platforms.

- **AI-Generated Art**: Create platforms where users can purchase unique AI-generated art or prints.

- **AI Apps**: Build and sell AI-driven apps for specific use cases, such as writing assistants, marketing tools, or personal productivity boosters.

Marketplaces for Selling AI Products and Services

Many marketplaces cater to digital products, and you can use these platforms to sell your AI-driven offerings. Popular marketplaces for selling AI services and products include:

- **Etsy**: For selling AI-generated artwork, designs, and digital assets.

- **App Stores**: For distributing AI-powered apps to a broad audience.

- **Udemy/Skillshare**: For offering AI-based courses or workshops to educate others on using AI tools.

- **Gumroad**: To sell templates, prompts, or digital products powered by generative AI.

14.2 Selling AI Art, Courses, Templates, and SaaS

Generative AI is a powerful tool for creators looking to monetize their work. Whether you're an artist, educator, or software developer, AI can be used to create valuable products and services that can be sold online.

Selling AI-Generated Art

 AI tools are transforming the art world, making it easier for artists to generate unique pieces that can be sold to collectors or used in commercial applications like advertising or design.

How to Monetize AI Art:

- **NFTs (Non-Fungible Tokens)**: Tokenize your AI-generated art and sell it on blockchain platforms like **OpenSea**, **Rarible**, or **Foundation**. This allows you to not only sell your artwork but also benefit from royalties whenever the art is resold.

- **Prints and Digital Downloads**: Offer AI-generated prints or digital downloads on platforms like **Etsy** or **Redbubble**. Artists can upload high-resolution AI art and sell it as posters, t-shirts, or other merchandise.

- **Commissions**: Offer personalized AI-generated art services for clients who want a custom piece tailored to their specifications.

Selling AI Courses

If you're proficient in using generative AI tools, you can monetize your expertise by creating and selling courses on platforms like **Udemy**, **Coursera**, or **Skillshare**.

Course Ideas:

- **AI Basics**: Teach beginners the fundamentals of generative AI, how it works, and its applications.

- **Tool-Specific Courses**: Create courses that focus on teaching users how to use specific AI tools such as **Midjourney**, **ChatGPT**, or **RunwayML**.

- **Advanced AI Techniques**: Offer more advanced courses on topics like **fine-tuning models**, **prompt engineering**, and integrating AI into business workflows.

Selling Templates and Prompts

AI templates and prompts are highly valuable for users who want to get started quickly or enhance their AI capabilities. Selling templates and curated prompts can be a profitable way to monetize generative AI.

Ways to Monetize Templates and Prompts:

- **Create Custom Templates**: Design and sell AI prompts or templates for specific use cases like blog writing, social media posts, product descriptions, or video scripts.

- **Prompt Packs**: Curate collections of high-quality, optimized prompts for AI writing tools, image generators, or chatbot builders and sell them on platforms like **Gumroad** or your own website.

- **Design Tools**: Sell pre-designed templates for tools like **Figma**, **Canva**, or **Photoshop**, which can be used in conjunction with AI-generated assets.

Selling SaaS Powered by AI

Building and selling SaaS (Software as a Service) products powered by generative AI is a lucrative avenue. These products often involve subscription models, which provide recurring income.

Examples of AI-Powered SaaS Products:

- **AI Copywriting Tools**: Create a SaaS platform that uses generative AI to help businesses generate content for blogs, social media, and email marketing.

- **Design Automation**: Develop a tool that uses AI to automate graphic design, video creation, or web design, allowing non-designers to create high-quality visuals easily.

- **AI-Powered Analytics**: Build a tool that uses AI to analyze data and generate actionable insights for businesses, like customer behavior or sales forecasting.

- **AI Virtual Assistants**: Create and sell AI-powered virtual assistants for businesses, helping them automate customer support, lead generation, or scheduling.

Summary: Monetizing with Gen AI

Generative AI offers a wide range of opportunities for monetization, from freelancing and consulting to selling products and services in digital marketplaces. Whether you are an artist, developer, educator, or entrepreneur, generative AI provides the tools to create innovative, valuable products that can be marketed and sold. By tapping into platforms like **Etsy**, **Udemy**, and **Gumroad**, or building your own SaaS products, you can leverage AI to create sustainable income streams in a rapidly growing industry.

Best Practices for Monetizing Generative AI:

- **Diversify your income streams**: Combine freelance work, product sales, and SaaS offerings to increase your earning potential.

- **Focus on value**: Ensure your products or services meet real needs in the market and provide clear value to your customers.

- **Stay ahead of the curve**: As AI technology evolves, continue learning and adapting to new tools and trends to stay competitive in the market.

14.3 Mini Case Study: From Side Hustle to Six Figures

In this section, we'll explore how one entrepreneur successfully transformed a generative AI side hustle into a six-figure business. This case study provides valuable insights into the practical steps, challenges, and strategies that helped turn a passion for AI into a thriving business.

Background:
 Sophia is a freelance graphic designer with a knack for creating digital art. She discovered **Midjourney** and **DALL·E** early on and began using these AI tools to create unique, high-quality art. Initially, she sold AI-generated prints on Etsy, but her sales were modest. Over time, she developed a deep understanding of AI's capabilities and expanded her business beyond art.

Key Milestones:

1. **Identifying a Niche**: Initially, Sophia offered generic AI art prints. After researching trends and customer preferences, she realized that there was a growing demand for **AI-generated digital art** for **branding and marketing purposes**. She shifted her focus to creating custom designs for businesses in the tech and startup sectors.

2. **Creating an Online Presence**: Sophia built a website showcasing her portfolio, alongside a blog and social media accounts that highlighted the potential of AI-generated designs. She also started offering **AI-powered design workshops** and **one-on-one consultations** to teach other designers and business owners how to use AI tools effectively.

3. **Diversifying Revenue Streams**: As her brand grew, Sophia expanded her offerings. She began creating **AI-generated logos**, **social media content packages**, and **email templates** for startups. She also began selling **AI prompts** and design templates for other digital creators and entrepreneurs. This diversification helped stabilize her income and attract a broader client base.

4. **Building a Community**: Sophia established a community of like-minded creators by hosting webinars, sharing tutorials, and offering a **membership program** where subscribers received exclusive AI prompts, templates, and behind-the-scenes design tips. This built a loyal following and created a steady stream of recurring income.

5. **Scaling with Outsourcing and SaaS**: Once Sophia's business hit the six-figure mark, she scaled by outsourcing certain tasks like customer support and marketing to freelancers. She also developed a **SaaS product** that allowed users to generate custom AI art with the click of a button. This product quickly gained traction in the design community.

Key Takeaways:

- **Niche Down**: Specializing in a specific market or product can help you stand out and attract high-value clients.

- **Diversify**: Multiple income streams, such as workshops, templates, and SaaS products, help stabilize and scale your business.

- **Community Building**: Establishing a loyal community can lead to recurring income and increased brand loyalty.

- **Scale Smartly**: Outsourcing and creating digital products (e.g., SaaS tools, templates) can help you scale without overextending yourself.

Sophia's success story illustrates how dedication, strategic thinking, and leveraging AI tools can transform a small side hustle into a highly profitable business.

14.4 Common Pitfalls & Best Practices

When monetizing your generative AI skills, it's essential to understand both the common pitfalls and the best practices to ensure long-term success. Here's a breakdown of the key dos and don'ts, so you can avoid mistakes and optimize your approach:

Common Pitfalls

1. **Over-Promising and Under-Delivering**

   Pitfall: Claiming results or outcomes that AI tools can't reliably produce can damage your reputation and harm client trust. Many AI tools are powerful but still have limitations (e.g., hallucinations, style inconsistencies, or technical restrictions).

   Solution: Be transparent with clients about what your AI services can and cannot do. Always set clear expectations to maintain client satisfaction.

2. **Neglecting Legal and Copyright Issues**

   Pitfall: Generating AI art, code, or text without properly understanding the intellectual property (IP) laws can lead to legal issues, especially when selling AI-generated works. Many platforms have ambiguous copyright policies.

   Solution: Always review the terms and conditions of the AI tools you use. For art, make sure you are clear on who owns the generated content—whether it's the AI provider, you, or the client. For software and code, ensure you respect licenses (e.g., MIT, Apache).

3. **Failing to Diversify Revenue Streams**

   Pitfall: Relying on just one product or service—like selling AI art on Etsy—can expose your business to market fluctuations. If a platform changes its policies or a trend fades, your income could take a significant hit.

   Solution: Diversify your income sources. Consider offering AI-driven services (e.g., consulting, customized prompts), selling digital products (templates, tools), and exploring new avenues such as SaaS.

4. **Inadequate Market Research**

   Pitfall: Launching AI-driven products or services without sufficient market research can lead to poor sales. Understanding market needs and your target audience is crucial.

Solution: Conduct thorough market research. Study trends, identify gaps, and understand the needs of your target market. Testing with small audiences and iterating on feedback is also essential.

5. **Not Investing in Marketing**

   Pitfall: Having a great product isn't enough if no one knows about it. Many creators neglect marketing, relying solely on word-of-mouth or organic traffic.

   Solution: Build a solid marketing plan that includes social media, SEO, email marketing, and collaborations with influencers or other creators. Invest time in promoting your work, even if it's a side hustle.

6. **Ignoring Customer Support and Experience**

   Pitfall: Poor customer support can quickly turn satisfied clients into unhappy ones. This is especially true when offering custom or high-value services.

   Solution: Provide excellent customer support. Set up automated systems for inquiries, offer clear communication about timelines, and follow up with clients to ensure they are satisfied with the product or service.

7. **Underpricing Your Services**

   Pitfall: Many creators start by underpricing their work to attract clients, but this can undervalue your skills and services. Over time, this practice can lead to burnout and decreased profitability.

   Solution: Start with competitive pricing, and as your expertise grows, increase your rates. Ensure your pricing reflects the value you offer and the quality of the work produced.

8. **Not Focusing on Continuous Learning**

   Pitfall: Generative AI is a rapidly evolving field, and failing to stay updated on the latest advancements can lead to outdated practices and missed opportunities.

   Solution: Regularly invest in learning. Participate in workshops, follow industry leaders, and continuously experiment with new tools and models. Staying updated ensures you remain competitive.

Best Practices for Monetizing with Generative AI

1. **Set Clear, Achievable Goals**

   Create a roadmap for your monetization journey. Set short-term and long-term goals, such as the number of clients you want per month or revenue targets. Tracking your progress will help you stay motivated and focused.

2. **Build a Strong Brand**

   Develop a brand that reflects your AI expertise. Whether it's through a portfolio website, social media, or a personal blog, showcase your best work, share insights, and build a community of followers who trust your expertise.

3. **Offer Free Value to Attract Leads**

   Create free content that provides value—this could be tutorials, sample templates, or AI prompt packs. Offering free resources can help you build an audience and convert them into paying customers.

4. **Leverage AI Communities and Networks**

   Engage with online communities focused on generative AI (e.g., Reddit, Discord, LinkedIn groups). Collaborate, share your work, and learn from others. Networking within the AI community can open doors to new opportunities and partnerships.

5. **Provide Custom Solutions and Personalization**

   Stand out by offering bespoke AI-driven solutions tailored to your clients' needs. Personalized services—such as creating custom AI art or designing unique workflows—can justify premium pricing and increase client loyalty.

6. **Iterate Based on Feedback**

   Continuously gather feedback from your clients, audience, and collaborators. Use this feedback to improve your products, services, and marketing efforts. Iteration helps you adapt to market changes and keep your offerings relevant.

7. **Focus on Quality over Quantity**

   In a crowded market, quality matters. Whether it's AI-generated art, written content, or code, delivering high-quality work will build trust and lead to repeat customers and referrals.

8. **Create Recurring Revenue Models**

   Subscription-based services or products (e.g., AI-generated content on a monthly basis, access to exclusive templates) can provide predictable and stable income. Consider implementing models that offer continuous value to your clients.

9. **Develop Partnerships and Collaborations**

   Collaborating with other creators, AI tool developers, or businesses can help expand your reach and access new markets. Strategic partnerships can provide joint marketing opportunities and attract new clients.

By avoiding these common pitfalls and implementing these best practices, you'll set yourself up for sustained success in monetizing your generative AI skills. Remember that building a business is a journey, and staying adaptable while focusing on delivering value to your audience is key to long-term success.

Chapter 15: Legal, Ethical & Societal Issues

15.1 Copyright, Fair Use, and Licensing

Generative AI raises significant questions about copyright, intellectual property (IP), and licensing because AI systems create content that can be identical to or inspired by human-made work. It's essential for creators and businesses to navigate these complexities to avoid legal disputes and ensure ethical practices.

Copyright Issues

- **Who Owns AI-Generated Content?**
  AI tools often create works based on existing datasets, and many jurisdictions are still grappling with whether AI can be considered an author. Some legal systems treat the user of AI as the creator, while others see AI-generated content as in the public domain, not subject to copyright.

- **Derivative Works**
  When using an AI model trained on copyrighted content (e.g., images, texts, music), the content it generates may be considered a derivative work. If the AI-generated content is too similar to the original work, it could potentially infringe on the copyright of the source material.

- **Solution:**
  Always ensure you have the right to use any datasets that your AI model is trained on. For AI creators, it's important to establish clear licensing terms for generated content, specifying who holds the copyright and how the content can be used.

Fair Use

- **What is Fair Use?**
  Fair use allows limited use of copyrighted material without permission, typically for

commentary, criticism, news reporting, research, or education. However, the boundaries of fair use are complex when it comes to AI-generated works.

- **Fair Use and AI**

  AI models may generate works that borrow heavily from copyrighted sources. Determining whether this falls under fair use requires careful consideration of factors like the purpose of use, the nature of the original work, and the effect on the market for the original.

- **Solution:**

  Always evaluate whether your use of AI-generated content aligns with fair use principles, especially when using copyrighted material. In cases of doubt, consult with an intellectual property lawyer.

Licensing

- **Licensing AI Models and Tools**

  When using AI platforms, it's essential to understand the licensing model of the AI tool or framework. Some tools offer open-source licenses, while others have restrictive terms (e.g., non-commercial use only). Ensure that the license aligns with your intended use, especially if you plan to commercialize AI-generated outputs.

- **Licensing Generated Content**

  When creating AI-generated works (e.g., art, music, code), you must decide how to license the resulting content. Many platforms and services provide specific licenses for AI-generated works (e.g., royalty-free, non-exclusive licenses).

- **Solution:**

  Familiarize yourself with the licensing terms of the AI tools and platforms you use. When selling or sharing AI-generated content, make sure the licenses are clear, and consider offering multiple licensing options to suit different uses.

15.2 Misinformation, Deepfakes, and Bias

Generative AI is a powerful tool, but its capabilities come with significant ethical and societal implications, particularly concerning misinformation, deepfakes, and bias. These issues have the potential to disrupt societies, affect public trust, and even cause harm to individuals and communities.

Misinformation

- **AI's Role in Misinformation**

  AI tools can generate realistic and convincing content, including fake news articles, social media posts, and videos. These AI-generated materials can be used to manipulate public opinion, spread false information, and disrupt democratic processes. The speed at which AI can create content amplifies the problem, as fake news spreads more quickly than traditional media.

- **Solutions to Combat Misinformation**

  - **Verification Tools**: Using AI to automatically verify the source and authenticity of content before it's disseminated.

  - **Content Moderation**: Platforms can implement AI-powered content moderation systems that flag or remove fake news or misleading information.

  - **Education**: Public awareness campaigns about the potential dangers of AI-generated misinformation can help mitigate its impact.

Deepfakes

- **What Are Deepfakes?**

  Deepfakes are AI-generated videos or audio that convincingly alter or fabricate a person's appearance, voice, or actions. While they have entertainment and artistic uses, deepfakes can also be used maliciously for fraud, defamation, or to spread misleading narratives.

- **Risks of Deepfakes**

  - **Political Manipulation**: Deepfakes can be used to impersonate politicians or public figures, causing harm to reputations or influencing public opinion.

  - **Identity Theft**: Deepfake technology can be used to impersonate individuals for fraudulent purposes, such as identity theft or scams.

  - **Public Trust**: The rise of deepfakes can erode public trust in media, as it becomes harder to distinguish between what's real and what's AI-generated.

- **Solutions to Combat Deepfakes**

  - **Detection Tools**: Developing AI systems capable of detecting deepfakes and flagging them on social media platforms, news outlets, and online videos.

  - **Legal Frameworks**: Governments can introduce laws that penalize the malicious use of deepfake technology, particularly for defamation, fraud, or political manipulation.

  - **Media Literacy**: Educating the public on how to recognize deepfakes and how to critically assess the authenticity of online content is critical.

Bias in AI

- **What Is AI Bias?**
  AI models are trained on data, and if that data is biased, the AI system will reflect and possibly exacerbate these biases. This can lead to discriminatory outcomes in various fields, such as hiring practices, criminal justice, lending, and healthcare.

- **Types of Bias**

- **Data Bias**: When training data is not representative of the population or contains prejudices.

- **Algorithmic Bias**: When algorithms unintentionally amplify biases in the data.

- **Representation Bias**: When certain groups (e.g., ethnic minorities, women) are underrepresented in training datasets, leading to inaccurate or unfair outcomes.

- **Examples of Bias in AI**

  - **Hiring Algorithms**: AI used for job recruitment may favor male candidates over female candidates if the training data is skewed toward male-dominated industries.

  - **Healthcare AI**: AI systems used to diagnose diseases may perform less accurately for underrepresented groups if they are trained on data from predominantly one demographic.

- **Solutions to Mitigate AI Bias**

  - **Diverse Training Data**: Ensuring that AI models are trained on diverse and representative datasets is key to reducing bias.

  - **Bias Audits**: Regular audits of AI systems by external experts to assess whether they are making biased decisions.

  - **Transparency and Accountability**: AI developers should prioritize transparency in their models and be accountable for any biases that are identified. Public documentation and open-source code can help address these concerns.

  - **Inclusive Design**: Involving diverse teams of researchers, developers, and stakeholders in AI development can help identify and mitigate biases early in the process.

Conclusion

The legal, ethical, and societal issues surrounding generative AI are complex and evolving. As creators, developers, and businesses engage with AI tools, it's crucial to stay informed about the implications of copyright, misinformation, bias, and deepfakes. By understanding these issues and implementing responsible practices, we can harness the power of AI while ensuring it serves society ethically and justly.

15.3 Responsible AI: Audits, Transparency, and Governance

As AI continues to evolve, it is essential to develop systems for ensuring the responsible use of generative AI, particularly in high-stakes applications like healthcare, law enforcement, and finance. Ethical guidelines, transparency, and governance structures are necessary to mitigate the risks associated with AI.

AI Audits

- **What is an AI Audit?**
  AI audits are systematic evaluations of AI systems to assess their performance, fairness, safety, and adherence to legal and ethical guidelines. Audits are crucial for identifying potential biases, inaccuracies, or unethical behaviors in AI systems.

- **Why Are AI Audits Important?**
  AI systems, especially generative models, can evolve in ways that are not always predictable. Audits help ensure that these systems remain aligned with human values and ethical standards. They can also ensure compliance with regulations and standards set by governing bodies.

- **How Are AI Audits Performed?**
  Audits often involve the following steps:

  1. **Model Transparency**: Review of the model's architecture, training data, and decision-making processes to ensure transparency.

2. **Bias Detection**: Analyzing the model's outcomes to identify and mitigate bias or discriminatory behavior.

3. **Compliance Checks**: Verifying the model's compliance with data privacy laws (such as GDPR) and other relevant regulations.

4. **Performance Monitoring**: Continuous evaluation of the model's effectiveness and its ability to adapt to new data.

- **Solution**

   Organizations can implement periodic AI audits, either internally or through third-party evaluators. These audits should be an ongoing process to adapt to new developments and potential ethical challenges.

Transparency

- **Why is Transparency Critical?**

   Transparency ensures that AI systems are understandable to stakeholders, including end users, regulators, and developers. When AI systems are transparent, their decisions, processes, and outcomes can be easily reviewed and challenged if necessary. Lack of transparency can breed distrust and make it difficult to resolve issues when they arise.

- **How to Achieve Transparency in AI**

   1. **Open Source Models**: Encourage the use of open-source AI models, where users can inspect the underlying code and training data.

   2. **Explainable AI**: Develop AI systems that offer insights into how decisions are made. This is especially crucial in sectors like healthcare and criminal justice, where AI recommendations can have serious consequences.

3. **Clear Documentation**: Provide clear documentation on model architecture, training processes, data sources, and known limitations.

- **Solution**

  Create standardized frameworks for transparency in AI. Regularly update users on how AI models evolve and disclose any changes made to the system's design or functionality.

AI Governance

- **What is AI Governance?**

  AI governance refers to the policies, regulations, and frameworks put in place to ensure that AI systems are developed and used responsibly. It encompasses a variety of factors, including ethical decision-making, accountability, data privacy, and user consent.

- **Why Is Governance Important?**

  Effective governance minimizes risks and ensures that AI technologies are used to promote social good. It also provides a framework for accountability and facilitates the integration of ethical considerations into AI design and deployment processes.

- **Governance Strategies**

  1. **Ethical Guidelines**: Organizations should establish a set of ethical guidelines that govern the development and use of AI systems.

  2. **Oversight Bodies**: Governments and independent organizations should create regulatory bodies to monitor AI technologies and their impact.

  3. **Accountability Frameworks**: Clear mechanisms for holding developers, organizations, and users accountable for any adverse impacts caused by AI systems.

- **Solution**

  Establish a balanced governance model that includes ethical guidelines, continuous oversight, and transparent accountability measures. Work with legal and regulatory bodies to develop international standards for AI governance.

15.4 Career Spotlight: AI Policy & Ethics Specialist

As AI technologies continue to advance, the demand for professionals who understand the ethical, legal, and societal implications of AI is on the rise. AI Policy & Ethics Specialists are crucial in shaping the future of AI in a way that is responsible, transparent, and aligned with human values.

Role of an AI Policy & Ethics Specialist

An AI Policy & Ethics Specialist works at the intersection of technology, law, and ethics. Their primary responsibilities include:

- **Developing Ethical Guidelines**: Ensuring that AI systems align with ethical standards and societal values.

- **Ensuring Regulatory Compliance**: Making sure AI technologies comply with relevant laws and regulations, including data privacy, intellectual property, and anti-discrimination laws.

- **Advocating for Fair Use**: Promoting fair and transparent use of AI technologies in industries such as healthcare, finance, and education.

- **Building Ethical Frameworks**: Developing frameworks for AI governance and oversight.

Key Skills

1. **Legal Knowledge**: A strong understanding of intellectual property law, data privacy, and regulatory frameworks like GDPR and CCPA.

2. **Ethical Understanding**: Expertise in ethical principles, such as fairness, accountability, and transparency in AI systems.

3. **Technology Acumen**: A working knowledge of how AI technologies function and how to assess their ethical implications.

4. **Communication Skills**: The ability to explain complex technical issues to non-technical stakeholders, including policymakers, businesses, and the public.

Career Path

AI Policy & Ethics Specialists can work in various settings, including:

- **Government Agencies**: Helping to develop regulations and policies for AI use at the national or international level.

- **Tech Companies**: Working within AI development teams to ensure ethical design and deployment of AI systems.

- **Consulting Firms**: Advising organizations on AI ethics and helping them navigate the complexities of AI technology in their operations.

- **Solution**
  This role offers a unique opportunity for individuals interested in both technology and social impact. To break into this field, gaining a background in law, computer science, or ethics, along with staying updated on the latest developments in AI, is essential.

15.5 Common Pitfalls & Best Practices

Common Pitfalls

1. **Lack of Transparency**: Failing to provide users and stakeholders with insights into how AI models make decisions.

2. **Ignoring Bias**: Overlooking biases in training data, which can lead to discriminatory AI outcomes.

3. **Unclear Legal Responsibility**: Not establishing clear lines of accountability when AI systems cause harm or make incorrect decisions.

4. **Misuse of AI**: Using AI in ways that exacerbate societal problems, such as spreading misinformation or creating deepfakes.

5. **Non-Compliance with Regulations**: Failing to stay updated on AI-related laws and regulations, leading to legal and reputational risks.

Best Practices

1. **Implement Ethical Audits**: Regularly audit AI systems for ethical alignment, bias, and fairness.

2. **Promote Transparency**: Make AI models as transparent as possible, providing explanations for their decisions.

3. **Foster Inclusivity**: Ensure that AI models are developed using diverse datasets that represent a wide range of demographics.

4. **Prioritize Accountability**: Hold developers and organizations accountable for the impact of their AI systems.

5. **Stay Informed on Regulations**: Keep up-to-date with evolving legal frameworks and ensure AI systems comply with them.

Solution

By adopting best practices, organizations and developers can build AI systems that are ethical, accountable, and fair. Regular audits, transparency, and compliance with regulations will go a long way in mitigating the risks associated with AI while maximizing its positive potential.

Chapter 16: Future pf Generative AI

16.1 AGI, Multi-Agent Systems, Personal AIs

The future of generative AI is rapidly evolving, moving from single-task models to complex ecosystems that simulate intelligence, autonomy, and collaboration at a scale never seen before. This chapter explores key directions such as Artificial General Intelligence (AGI), multi-agent architectures, and the rise of personalized AI companions.

Artificial General Intelligence (AGI)

- **Definition**:

   AGI refers to a type of AI that possesses the general cognitive capabilities of a human, capable of reasoning, problem-solving, learning, and adapting across diverse domains — not just narrow, task-specific functions like today's generative models.

- **How It Differs from Current AI**:

Capability	Narrow AI (Today)	AGI (Future)
Task scope	Single domain	Multi-domain
Adaptability	Pre-trained knowledge	Learns continuously
Creativity	Pattern-based	Abstract, original thought

Memory	Short-lived context	Long-term knowledge

-

  Key Indicators of AGI Progress:

    - Reasoning across disciplines

    - Long-term memory and learning

    - Transfer of knowledge between unrelated tasks

    - Self-directed goal-setting

- **Ethical & Societal Implications**:

    - Power asymmetry between creators and users

    - Human-level decision-making without accountability

    - Need for strict governance and control systems

Multi-Agent Systems

- **Definition**:
  Multi-agent systems involve a network of AI agents that communicate, collaborate, or compete to perform tasks. Unlike single large models, these systems specialize and delegate tasks intelligently, often improving efficiency and autonomy.

- **Examples of Use Cases**:

- **Autonomous research assistants**: One agent summarizes documents, another designs experiments, a third checks for ethical compliance.

- **AI project managers**: Coordinating different AI tools like text generators, image creators, and code builders.

- **Simulated societies**: Using agents to simulate economic, political, or social behavior for forecasting or training.

How They Work:

[Planner Agent] → delegates task →

[Text Agent] → creates prompt →

[Code Agent] → builds script →

[Evaluator Agent] → checks output →

[Feedback Agent] → updates process

- **Benefits**:

  - Modular and scalable

  - Reduces complexity through specialization

  - Enables emergent intelligence through collaboration

Personal AIs

- **Definition**:
  Personal AIs are generative systems tailored to an individual's data, preferences, style, and objectives. They act like intelligent digital companions, assistants, or even co-creators.

- **Applications**:

  - Personal health advisors

  - AI writing and coaching partners

  - Family historians and memory curators

  - Autonomous business agents managing your tools

- **Key Features**:

  - **Persistent memory**: Remembers user history, tone, and preferences

  - **Adaptability**: Evolves with the user

  - **Proactive**: Can anticipate needs and suggest actions

Example:

You: "Help me plan a weekly meal based on my health goals."

Your AI: "Based on your recent workout routine and calorie preferences, here's a high-protein meal plan with a shopping list and optional vegan swaps."

- **Challenges**:

  - Privacy and data protection

  - Platform lock-in and lack of portability

  - Risk of over-dependence or echo chambers

Key Takeaways

Concept	Description
AGI	General intelligence across all domains, surpassing narrow AI
Multi-Agent Systems	Teams of AI agents working together for scalable intelligence
Personal AIs	Tailored assistants that learn and evolve with the user

Practice Activity

Scenario: Imagine you are designing a personal AI that helps a creative entrepreneur manage content creation, customer support, and scheduling.

- List 3 agents you would create.

- Describe how they would collaborate.

- Suggest one safeguard you'd implement to ensure responsible use.

16.2 Open vs Closed AI: The Ecosystem Debate

The generative AI landscape is sharply divided between **open-source** and **closed/proprietary** approaches. This debate goes beyond just code accessibility—it touches on innovation, safety, ethics, and control over the future of artificial intelligence.

Closed AI Ecosystems

Definition: Proprietary models developed by private companies with limited access to weights, data, or internal architecture.

Examples: OpenAI's GPT-4/5, Anthropic's Claude 3, Google's Gemini Ultra, Mistral Large (commercial license).

Advantages:

- Advanced performance due to extensive compute resources and data

- Controlled releases reduce misuse (e.g., alignment, filtering)

- Easier to productize and scale commercially

Concerns:

- Lack of transparency in data sources and safety claims

- Risk of monopolization and "black box" decision-making

- Limited ability for community audit or collaboration

Open AI Ecosystems

Definition: Models with public access to training weights, code, documentation, and community-driven improvements.

Examples: Meta's LLaMA family, Mistral 7B, Falcon, BLOOM, OpenBioLLM

Advantages:

- Transparency and community accountability

- Accelerated innovation via open experimentation

- Accessible to startups, researchers, and low-resource regions

Concerns:

- Increased misuse risk (e.g., deepfakes, bias propagation)

- Fragmentation in safety standards

- Difficulty in ensuring responsible deployment at scale

Comparison Table

Feature	Open AI (e.g., LLaMA)	Closed AI (e.g., GPT-4)
Transparency	High	Low
Customization	High	Limited
Safety Controls	Community-driven	Centralized, proprietary
Cost	Lower (often free)	Higher (pay-per-use or licensing)
Innovation Speed	Rapid, community-driven	Focused, structured
Risk of Misuse	Higher	Moderated by usage policies

Philosophical Tension

The debate parallels earlier tech shifts:

- **Open Source Software vs Proprietary Software**

- **Wikipedia vs Encyclopedias**

- **Linux vs Windows**

Now, it's about who gets to build, own, and guide the future of machine intelligence.

Hybrid Approach: The Middle Path

- Many companies are opting for **"open-weight but licensed"** models.

- Examples: Meta's LLaMA under controlled terms, Mistral's mix of open/closed releases.

- Tool builders are using **open backends** (like Ollama, LangChain) while leveraging **closed APIs** (like OpenAI) for critical features.

Key Takeaways

Concept	Insight
Closed AI	High performance, strong safety, limited transparency
Open AI	Transparent and customizable, but harder to govern
Future Trend	Hybrid ecosystems balancing openness and responsibility

Practice Activity

Debate Prompt:
You are consulting a startup. They must choose between using GPT-4 (closed) or LLaMA 3 (open) for their AI product.

- Write down 2 benefits and 2 risks for each.

- Based on your product goals (e.g., privacy, cost, innovation), choose one and justify it.

16.3 Emerging Models: GPT-5, Claude 3, Gemini Ultra, etc.

The newest generation of generative AI models is reshaping what's possible—pushing boundaries in reasoning, memory, interactivity, and multi-modal abilities. Here's a look at the front-runners shaping the future.

GPT-5 (OpenAI)

- **Status**: Anticipated or in private testing stages

- **Strengths**:

  - Improved reasoning and contextual understanding

  - Potential for native multi-modality (text, image, audio, video)

  - Stronger tool-use and long-term memory features

- **Use Cases**: Advanced agents, real-time tutoring, creative co-pilots

---

Claude 3 (Anthropic)

- **Versions**: Claude 3 Haiku (fast), Sonnet (balanced), Opus (most powerful)

- **Strengths**:

  - Ethical alignment and low hallucination rates

  - Long-context memory (up to 200K+ tokens)

  - Strong performance in reasoning tasks

- **Use Cases**: Legal research, coding, enterprise tools, policy drafting

---

Gemini Ultra (Google DeepMind)

- **Strengths**:

  - Trained from the ground up for multi-modality

  - Integration with Google Workspace and search

  - Superior in math, science, and technical reasoning

- **Use Cases**: Data science, search agents, media creation

Mistral & Mixtral

- **Open Models**: Mistral 7B, Mixtral 8x7B (Mixture-of-Experts)

- **Strengths**:

    - Fast, efficient, high-quality open weights

    - Easy to run locally with Ollama or LM Studio

- **Use Cases**: On-device inference, private AI apps, embedded agents

---

LLaMA 3 (Meta)

- **Strengths**:

    - Open-weight models with high performance

    - Strong multilingual capabilities

    - Community-driven ecosystem with rapid iteration

- **Use Cases**: Custom LLMs, local deployment, research

Tool Comparison Table

Model	Type	Context Length	Modality	Open/Closed	Key Strengths
GPT-5	Proprietary	TBD (Very High)	Multi-modal	Closed	Tool-use, reasoning,

					agent workflows
Claude 3 Opus	Proprietary	200K+	Text	Closed	Alignment, low hallucination
Gemini Ultra	Proprietary	1M+ (planned)	Multi-modal	Closed	Search, science, technical tasks
Mistral/Mixtral	Open	32K+	Text	Open	Efficiency, local deployment
LLaMA 3	Open	8K–65K+	Text	Open	Custom fine-tuning, low-cost access

Key Takeaways

Insight	Description
New models are multi-modal	Capable of handling text, images, video, and code together

Open models are catching up	Mistral and LLaMA 3 are closing the performance gap
Context length matters	Enables long documents, memory, and detailed reasoning

Practice Activity

Scenario: You are designing an AI tutor.
Evaluate which model would be best suited for:

- Real-time math explanation

- In-depth textbook summarization

- Private deployment in a classroom

List your top two choices and explain why.

16.4 Expert Predictions: 2030 and Beyond

By 2030, generative AI is expected to become deeply integrated into our lives—transforming industries, redefining creativity, and reshaping society. Here's a synthesis of predictions from top AI experts and thought leaders.

1. Ubiquitous Personal AIs

- Everyone may have a **personal AI agent**—tailored to their habits, communication style, goals, and privacy needs.

- These agents will manage email, learning, shopping, and even emotional support.

Quote:

"AI won't just answer your questions—it will anticipate them and act before you even ask."
— Mustafa Suleyman, CEO of Inflection AI

---

2. AI as Infrastructure

- Gen AI will become the **invisible infrastructure** of the digital world:

  - Embedded in cars, homes, cities, and wearables

  - Powering decisions, services, and personalization everywhere

---

3. Rise of Multi-Agent Systems

- Future AI systems may consist of **collaborative agent swarms**:

  - One agent plans, another researches, another executes

  - Applications: AI research teams, robotic systems, decentralized control

---

4. Human-AI Co-Creation Becomes the Norm

- Creative workflows will evolve into **"AI-native" collaboration environments**.

- Writers, artists, coders, and educators will **co-create** with AI across modalities.

---

5. Regulation and Rights Frameworks Will Mature

- Countries will implement **AI rights charters**, **audit standards**, and **AI licensing models**.

- Debates will center on:

    - AI personhood

    - Synthetic media labeling

    - Data and model ownership

---

6. AGI and the Alignment Question

- Many experts believe **Artificial General Intelligence (AGI)** could emerge by 2030 or shortly after.

- Key concerns:

    - Ensuring alignment with human values

    - Preventing runaway self-improvement

- Balancing open research and security

Quote:

"We must build AI not just to be intelligent, but to be wise."
— Fei-Fei Li, Stanford AI Lab

Technological Forecast Table

Domain	2030 Prediction
Education	AI tutors with empathy and multi-lingual fluency
Healthcare	AI-powered diagnostics, therapy, and personal health agents
Creative Work	Real-time video creation from text, virtual co-authors
Economy	New job classes: AI conductors, synthetic media directors
Society	Widespread AI norms, ethics councils, cultural adaptation

Practice Activity

Imagine it's the year 2030. Draft a one-day timeline showing how a typical person might use AI from morning to night. Focus on how it assists, learns, and interacts throughout their day.

16.5 Common Pitfalls & Best Practices

Pitfall	How to Avoid It
Overestimating short-term potential	Ground expectations—adoption and integration take time
Relying on a single AI model	Use diverse models to avoid blind spots and maximize results
Ignoring ethical and societal consequences	Stay informed on legal, cultural, and safety debates
Lack of AI literacy among leadership and teams	Invest in ongoing AI education and cross-functional upskilling
Building without user alignment or real needs	Co-create with users and test iteratively
Treating AI as "just another tool"	Approach it as a collaborator, not just a service

Key Takeaways

- The future is not just AI-powered—it's **AI-integrated**.

- Co-evolution of humans and AI will define new cultural norms, workflows, and value systems.

- Ethical, creative, and strategic thinking will matter as much as technical skill.

Part VI: Resources and Roadmaps

Appendix A: AI Glossary

Term	Definition
Generative AI	A type of AI that creates new content such as text, images, music, or code.
LLM (Large Language Model)	A neural network trained on massive amounts of text to understand and generate human-like language.
Transformer	A model architecture enabling parallel processing and long-range dependencies in text.
Prompt Engineering	Crafting inputs to elicit desired outputs from AI models.
Fine-tuning	Adapting a pre-trained model to specific tasks or domains using additional data.
Inference	The process of running a trained model to generate predictions or outputs.
GAN (Generative Adversarial Network)	A model that uses two networks (generator and discriminator) to generate realistic data.

Diffusion Models	Models that create images by reversing a noise process over many steps.
Embedding	A numeric representation of data (e.g., text) for similarity comparison.
Vector Database	A type of database optimized for storing and querying vector embeddings.
RAG (Retrieval-Augmented Generation)	A technique where AI retrieves external data to improve output accuracy.
API (Application Programming Interface)	A way for software components to communicate with each other.
No-Code/Low-Code	Platforms that allow building applications without or with minimal coding.
Agent	A dynamic AI entity capable of autonomous decisions and actions.
Hallucination (AI)	When an AI generates factually incorrect or nonsensical output.

Bias (AI)	Systematic errors in model predictions due to skewed training data.

Appendix B: Prompt Engineering Cheat Sheets

1. Writing Prompt Template

Act as a [role]. Write a [type of content] on [topic] with a tone that is [tone]. Include [specific elements].

Example:

Act as a content strategist. Write a blog post on sustainable fashion with an inspiring tone. Include stats and a call to action.

---

2. Summarization Prompt Template

Summarize the following text in [X] bullet points. Focus on [purpose: key ideas, decisions, outcomes].

Example:

Summarize this article in 5 bullet points. Focus on key findings and implications for educators.

---

3. Coding Assistant Prompt Template

Help me write a [type of script] in [language] that does the following: [describe function]. Also, explain the code.

Example:

Write a Python script that scrapes job listings from a webpage and outputs them to CSV. Explain each part of the code.

---

4. Creative Prompt Template

Generate a [genre] story about [subject/theme]. Use [tone/style]. Include [characters/conflict/resolution].

Example:

Generate a short science fiction story about climate change. Use a reflective tone and include a human-AI alliance.

---

5. Chatbot Personality Template

Act as a chatbot with the following traits: [traits]. Use [language/tone]. Always [key behaviors].

Example:

Act as a friendly productivity coach. Use encouraging language. Always ask what the user wants to prioritize today.

Appendix C: Tool Comparison Charts by Domain

1. Text Generation Tools

Tool	Strengths	Ideal Use Case	Pricing	Notable Limits
ChatGPT (OpenAI)	Conversational, coding, writing	General-purpose assistant	Freemium	May hallucinate facts
Claude (Anthropic)	Long context, safe outputs	Sensitive or structured writing	Freemium/Paid	Slower release cycle
Gemini (Google)	Integrated search + writing	Research-enhanced writing	Freemium	Variable output style
Jasper	Marketing, SEO focus	Branding, ads, sales copy	Paid	Costly for casual use

2. Image Generation Tools

Tool	Strengths	Best Use Case	Customization	Pricing
Midjourney	High aesthetics, detailed	Art, branding, fantasy	Moderate	Paid
DALL·E	Edit + generate, OpenAI native	Blog images, creative ideas	High	Freemium
Stable Diffusion	Open-source, customizable	Local/private model use	Very High	Free (local)

3. Audio & Music Tools

Tool	Strengths	Use Case	Voice Cloning?	Pricing
Aiva	Composing for film/games	Instrumental background music	No	Freemium/Paid
Soundraw	Royalty-free compositions	YouTube, content creation	No	Paid

ElevenLabs	High-quality voice synthesis	Audiobooks, narration	Yes	Freemium/Paid

4. Video Generation Tools

Tool	Strengths	Best For	Avatar Support	Pricing
Synthesia	Corporate, multilingual avatars	Training, corporate videos	Yes	Paid
Pictory	Text to video summarization	Blogs to video, summaries	No	Freemium
RunwayML	Real-time video editing	Creative production, VFX	No	Freemium/Paid

5. Code and Automation Tools

Tool	Strengths	Best For	No-Code Support	Pricing
GitHub Copilot	Context-aware code generation	IDE-based coding help	No	Paid
Replit AI	Live code generation	Fast prototyping, collaboration	Partial	Freemium
n8n	Workflow automation	Custom backend automation	Yes	Open-source
DeepAgent	AI agents + no-code builder	AI-powered apps	Yes	Paid

Appendix D: Code Snippets, Templates, and Workflows

1. Code Snippet: Text Summarization with OpenAI API (Python)

```python
import openai


openai.api_key = "your-api-key"


response = openai.ChatCompletion.create(
  model="gpt-4",
  messages=[{"role": "user", "content": "Summarize this article..."}]
)


print(response['choices'][0]['message']['content'])
```

Use: Summarize large bodies of text using GPT-4.

---

2. Template: AI Writing Prompt for Blogs

Act as a tech blogger. Write a 1000-word article about [topic] targeting [audience]. Use a tone that is [friendly/informative]. Include:

- Introduction

- Problem statement

- Data/statistics

- Solution

- CTA

---

3. n8n Workflow: Email Summarizer Bot

Steps Overview (text-based flowchart):

Trigger (New Email)

|

Extract Email Text

|

Send to OpenAI Node (Summarize)

|

Send Summary via Telegram/Slack

---

4. Bubble Template: Customer Feedback Analyzer

- Input form for feedback

- Backend workflow triggers sentiment analysis

- Dashboard shows aggregate sentiments and suggestions

---

5. LangChain RAG Flow (Text-Based)

User Query

|

Vector Store (FAISS, Chroma)

|

Retrieve Top 5 Docs

|

Prompt LLM with Context

|

LLM Output

Appendix E: Career Paths & Certification Roadmaps

1. Career Path: AI Product Manager

Skills Needed:

- Understanding of AI concepts and models

- Project management and agile methodologies

- User experience (UX) design

- Business strategy and product lifecycle

Certification & Courses:

- **AI Product Manager by Product School**

- **AI For Everyone by Andrew Ng (Coursera)**

- **Product Management with AI (LinkedIn Learning)**

Typical Roles:

- Product Manager for AI tools or platforms

- Technical Program Manager

- AI Solutions Architect

2. Career Path: AI Research Scientist

Skills Needed:

- Advanced knowledge in machine learning and deep learning

- Experience with neural networks, transformers, GANs, and more

- Strong background in mathematics (calculus, statistics, linear algebra)

- Python and research-oriented tools (e.g., TensorFlow, PyTorch)

Certification & Courses:

- **Deep Learning Specialization by Andrew Ng (Coursera)**

- **AI Researcher Nanodegree (Udacity)**

- **Master's or Ph.D. in AI-related fields**

Typical Roles:

- Research Scientist at AI-focused companies

- Machine Learning Engineer

- AI Algorithm Developer

3. Career Path: AI Developer (Software Engineer)

Skills Needed:

- Proficiency in programming languages such as Python, Java, and C++

- Familiarity with machine learning libraries and frameworks (e.g., scikit-learn, TensorFlow, PyTorch)

- Experience with cloud platforms (AWS, Google Cloud, Azure)

- Ability to deploy models and integrate them into applications

Certification & Courses:

- **AI Programming with Python by Udacity**

- **AWS Certified Machine Learning – Specialty**

- **Microsoft Certified: Azure AI Engineer**

Typical Roles:

- AI Developer at tech companies

- AI Solutions Engineer

- AI Backend Developer

4. Career Path: AI Ethics & Policy Specialist

Skills Needed:

- Strong understanding of AI and its societal impacts

- Legal and ethical principles in technology

- Policy writing and advocacy

- Communication skills for educating the public and stakeholders

Certification & Courses:

- **AI Ethics & Society (Harvard Online)**

- **Responsible AI Certification by Microsoft**

- **AI Policy & Governance (University of California)**

Typical Roles:

- AI Ethics Researcher

- Policy Advisor for AI Regulation

- Corporate Ethics Officer in AI-related companies

---

5. Career Path: AI Entrepreneur/Startup Founder

Skills Needed:

- Knowledge of AI tools and applications

- Business development and venture capital

- Marketing and scaling AI products

- Problem-solving and innovative thinking

Certification & Courses:

- **AI Entrepreneurship by Stanford**

- **StartUp School (Y Combinator)**

- **AI for Entrepreneurs (Udemy)**

Typical Roles:

- Founder/CEO of AI startups

- AI Consultant for businesses

- Product Development Lead in startups

---

6. Career Path: AI Content Creator & Educator

Skills Needed:

- Ability to simplify complex AI concepts

- Video content creation (YouTube, TikTok, etc.)

- Course development (Udemy, Teachable)

- Engagement on social media platforms

Certification & Courses:

- **AI Educator Certifications (LinkedIn Learning)**

- **Create and Teach AI Courses (Udemy)**

- **AI in Education (MIT OpenCourseWare)**

Typical Roles:

- AI YouTuber/Content Creator

- Online AI Course Instructor

- Author/Blog Writer on AI-related topics